RUNNING TO EXTREMES

LISA TAMATI

ALLEN&UNWIN

SYDNEY · MELBOURNE · AUCKLAND · LONDON

This edition published in 2013
First published in 2012

Allen & Unwin
Level 3, 228 Queen Street
Auckland 1010, New Zealand
Phone: (64 9) 377 3800

83 Alexander Street
Crows Nest NSW 2065, Australia
Phone: (61 2) 8425 0100
Email: info@allenandunwin.com
Web: www.allenandunwin.com

Cataloguing-in-Publication details are available
from the National Library of Australia
www.trove.nla.gov.au

ISBN 978 1 74331 764 8

Set in Apollo MT by Post Pre-press Group, Australia
Printed in Australia by McPherson's Printing Group

10 9 8 7 6 5 4 3 2 1

MIX
Paper from
responsible sources
FSC
www.fsc.org   FSC® C001695

The paper in this book is FSC® certified.
FSC® promotes environmentally responsible,
socially beneficial and economically viable
management of the world's forests.

RUNNING TO EXTREMES

Contents

For Jane Dick,
with thoughts of Tanglang La

Sport has the power to change the world. It has the power to unite in a way that little else does. It speaks to youth in a language they understand. Sport can create hope where once there was only despair. It is more powerful than governments in breaking down racial barriers. It laughs in the face of all types of discrimination.

Nelson Mandela

Foreword

In today's busy and constantly changing world, time seems to fly faster than it has ever before. We all have so much going on, as parents, partners, employees or business owners, that we let individual goals fade as we convince ourselves that it is OK to let our dreams slide. Between the kids and working to earn an income in order to meet the mortgage payments to house the family, it's easy to sacrifice your own goals, no matter how big or small they may be.

When I entered my forties I was a professional chef, dedicated mother and partner and I felt I had no choice but to deal with, manage and accept my daily commitments, while accepting that the goals I had set myself in earlier years were now out of reach. I began to believe that I was no longer an individual who could tick some pretty cool boxes and say 'I've done it!' while still being able to maintain my commitment to my family and my work.

I had an adventurous upbringing, sailing the Pacific with my father for many years, being home schooled and experiencing one adventure after another. After settling in New Zealand my focus became my work and my family. So here I was, once adventurer sailing the world with Dad to now being content with the white picket fence, children and a dog.

Don't get me wrong, my two children are wonderful and I love my brilliantly crazy husband. But three years ago, I realised I had more within me and that I needed to set myself some new goals. I had to achieve new things.

I went into a bookshop initially seeking a good romantic novel for comfort. But I stumbled across Lisa's first book, *Running Hot*. The cover won me over and I flicked through a few pages. A feeling of excitement came over me, while a fear within me tried to stop me reading more. The book, at that stage, was way out of my comfort zone. But I kept flicking and Lisa's book won over the romantic novel.

Having read and re-read the book several times, it inspired me to break out of my contented mould and set out to remould the true me. What would these new goals be? Maybe run a half marathon? Could I complete a full marathon? After all, what Lisa had achieved was unbelievable and super human and way out of the reach of a mere mortal like myself. And yet, it was so inspirational that it sparked me into action to at least set and chase a goal for myself.

I began to walk in the evenings. Then five months later I entered a 5km fun run with my two boys. I then targeted and completed a half marathon. It was tough—very tough. I was full of excuses and wanted to give up, but I kept telling myself if Lisa can run an entire desert, then surely I can run a half marathon with aid stations every few kilometres. And I did it.

Then off I went in search of a marathon to run. Then another. And another. Within three years of that bookshop visit, I entered my first ultramarathon—a 100-kilometre challenge. But not just any ultramarathon—the Northburn 100, organised by none other than Lisa herself.

I felt compelled to be present, at least to meet my mentor and inspiration. Knowing it was a 'Lisa Race', a race where you HAVE to leave all day-to-day gripes at the gate, where you dig deep, aim high and reach into your true soul to be yourself, to be at your very best to at least survive, let alone complete the event, I had to be part of it.

I was full of fear, yet also overwhelming excitement, reflecting how I felt three years earlier when I first picked up Lisa's book knowing it may change my life and really stretch my boundaries, to truly challenge my comfort zone, and make me think I was crazy.

This event is unlike any other. The 'Super Warrior' participants, the support crews, the families, fans and spectators create a community of like-minded people that I never knew existed. There is a huge world out there full of adventurous people, like I once was, and I am screaming loudly to say I have now become one of those people again—people that love life, family and friends, but are not scared to take a moment, or a few days, to complete a mere 160-kilometre run through some of the toughest terrain in the world, to simply say 'I did it!' Or 'I gave it my best shot!'

So it is thanks to you, Lisa, that I have reignited that belief within myself, to know I can do it if I wish to and to know that doing it will not put pressure on what means most to me—my family and friends—but that it will make us all the richer for being part of it.

Thanks, Lisa . . . you are an inspiration to all! May this book serve to others as the driver in lifting life and self-belief as your first book did for me.

Virginia Winstone

Introduction

Never give up. If you're not running, walk. If you're not walking, crawl. Never stop moving forward.

Dean Karnazes

Our sport is extreme. Some say we are crazy. Others ask why we do it to ourselves. We are a strange breed and we come from all walks of life and all professions, all ethnicities and religions. In a race we are all equal. We race in deserts, in the mountains, through forested woodlands, through jungles and even, if need be, on the road. Some of us run in circles around 1- or 2-kilometre circuits for hours or days or, even, weeks on end. We have been known to cross entire countries, even entire continents. One or two of us have even run around the entire earth.

Our races start at 50 kilometres, a little beyond the marathon distance, and go up to 5000 kilometres or even more on occasion. Sometimes we have crews who cater to our every need but, more often than not, we have to carry all we need for the day or the week on our backs. We seek out extreme landscapes and extreme temperatures from the Antarctic to the Sahara.

A hardy bunch who like to push the limits—the limits of human endurance, our own physical limits, our willpower, our resolve to achieve what we have set out to do—we will go to extreme lengths and overcome huge obstacles to avoid a 'did not finish.'

Some of us are extremely talented athletes, others are of average ability, still others have disabilities, but we all want the same thing: to complete the challenges we set for ourselves. I have seen a blind man run the Moroccan Sahara and a man with only one leg beat me to the finish line in Death Valley. I have seen a man with one arm and one leg run across a desert and another 75-year-old man finish the so-called 'toughest race on earth'. I have seen a number of runners who have had broken backs fight to come back and run desert races. I have seen a woman with multiple sclerosis complete more than 250 kilometres with the help of a pair of crutches. Asthmatics, epileptics, runners who have had hip replacements, heart attack victims . . . the list goes on.

We are often eccentric, or have fiercely held beliefs. I have seen a man dressed in a rhino suit do the Marathon des Sables in Morocco to draw attention to the plight of rhinoceroses. I have seen two young boys with cerebral palsy carried over 240 kilometres by a group of dedicated runners who wanted them to experience a multi-day stage race. In another desert race, a runner completed the course dressed as a waiter while carrying a tray in one hand with a bottle of Coke. Many of us run for our chosen charities and try to contribute to the world in what little way we can by raising money and awareness.

There are more of us now than there ever have been before. We come from every nation in the world and we all strive to go beyond what was once considered the ultimate endurance test by running extreme distances in extreme landscapes.

We have a collective need for adventure, to find out what sort of stuff we are made of, to be the best we can be, to give something our all. Our driving forces and our motivations are varied and each of us has our own story to tell. We are all without exception hardworking, determined souls. We have to be—we are ultramarathon runners.

That one question

There's one question I get asked by nearly everyone I meet. It's the one thing they all want to know and the one question I find difficult to answer quickly and succinctly. It is, of course, 'Why do you do it?'

Those five words are really loaded. What I think most people who ask me that mean is something along these lines:

'Why don't you just give up when the going gets so tough most people would just lie down and cry? Why can you push through pain barriers, and beat all odds, continue on for hours or days in a state of exhaustion that most humans would never conceive as possible, through sleep deprivation, hallucinations, blisters, shin splints, inflammation, digestion problems and altered mental states? Why, after swearing black and blue you will never do it again, do you turn up at the next race all excited and ready to go?'

Needless to say, I've given this a lot of thought over the years. I think every ultramarathon runner would answer the question differently but there are several things that drive me to run.

For most of us, our world today is so comfortable, so physically soft, and at the same time so terribly demanding and stressful that it can be hard to keep up with everything we feel we need to do in a day. For me, running helps regain a healthy balance between my mind, my body and my soul—that is why I do it.

It takes real discipline to train for an event, and then to give my absolute all in order to finish that race. With every race I enter, I know I am risking failure but I also have the confidence in myself to know that I will push myself to my very limits in the pursuit of success.

I love single-mindedly pursuing a goal. I find having a singular goal is quite purifying because there's so much going on in my life in terms of commitments and expectations—the phone's constantly ringing, emails are coming in, there are a hundred things that need doing—and I have to find a way to balance it all. But when I go to a race, I leave all that behind and I just focus on the trail.

When I go to a race, I don't enjoy the pain of it—absolutely not—but I enjoy the focus that it gives me. While I'm racing, my mind is constantly preoccupied with taking the next step. I know I can't let go for a minute, especially in desert races or when I'm running through the night. I've got to be watching where I'm going. I've got to be aware of how much fluid I've taken in. I need to know how many calories I've eaten. I've got to be listening to my body and where the pain is. I need to know how my mates I'm running with are doing. I need to worry about whether I need to be motivating them or if they are motivating me. My whole focus around the clock is on getting to the finish line.

It can be extremely tiring because there's no down time, even in the stage races, although there's always the relief of getting to camp when I know I'll be spending the night there. We sit around sharing war stories about what we've gone through that day. But the whole time we're all still focused on that goal of making the finish line. The rewards for all that hard work are the sense of pride, of achievement, of tired satisfaction, and of confidence that come from crossing that finish line.

Another thing I love about ultrarunning is that when some-one is challenged in such an extreme way, both mentally and physically, you get to see the true essence of that person. I think that's something a lot of us want to do—to get to that point in a race, adventure or expedition where we've got nothing left, where we're totalled and we've given everything but we somehow man-age to pull something out of ourselves to keep going. That's what most of us want to find out. Have we got that in us? Can we push it that little bit harder? What mettle are we made of?

Through the sport, I have really learned to value people who push themselves beyond normal barriers and overcome obstacles. For me, it's not about being the fastest on the course—that doesn't impress me. It's the guy who is last, it's the girl who has broken her back and has fought back and now she's crossing the desert, or the 75-year-old who's com-ing back into the desert for the fifteenth time and he won't let anyone tell him he can't do it. Those are the stories that I really love and that's what I love about the ultramarathon scene as opposed to the more competitive marathon and triathlon scenes. There it's all about competing against each other. Our sport does have an element of that, but at the end of the day most of us are in to compete against and test ourselves.

The power of running to change people's lives, to put people's lives back together and to help rebuild their self-esteem is another reason I do it. You go through hardships in running but that makes you tougher and shows you what is important in life. It takes you back to basics. You can't be an ultramarathon runner and really arrogant because you're dealing with Mother Nature, and Mother Nature will always give you a hiding. She will also show you your strengths and your vulnerabilities, your extra-ordinary abilities and your inherent human weaknesses.

1
Return to Death Valley

I think better when I'm running. My soul is at its quietest when I'm in movement.

Badwater Ultramarathon, 13–14/7/2009

The Badwater Ultramarathon in Death Valley is one of those things it's hard to do just once. It's such a cool event that I couldn't wait to go back the following year to improve my time. It's almost like the unofficial world champs, it's such a big event. I ran it for the first time in 2008 and in 2009 I really wanted to go back again—I hadn't had enough.

Described as 'the world's toughest foot race', Badwater is a 217-kilometre non-stop race which starts 86 metres below sea level in California's Death Valley. From there, it climbs up 2548 metres to the finish line on Mount Whitney. Taking place each year in mid-July, the weather conditions are extreme and the temperature reaches over 49° Celsius even in the shade.

Entry into the race has always been by invitation only

but I knew that having run it once, I'd still have to reapply and hope like hell I'd be invited back. Even now, after doing the race twice, I'd still like to go back again but there are so many other events I'd like to do as well that I have to pick and choose—it's such an expensive undertaking to go from New Zealand to Death Valley with all the crew.

After running the race the previous year, I knew I had to pull together a fantastic crew to come with me. After a few hiccups, the team finally came together. I wanted to have my ex-husband (and fellow ultrarunner) Gerhard Lusskandl crew for me again but he had already decided that he wanted to run the race, too, this time. With us both being there, it made sense to share crew accommodation and logistics, which was great. It made things a bit cheaper for both of us.

I managed to convince Murray Dick from Taranaki Engineering to sponsor me, and once he was on board he proved to be a brilliant supporter. He's a real adventurer and a real Taranaki stalwart. He loves a huge challenge. In his fifties, Murray decided that he wanted to come with me and run 10 kilometres alongside me at some point during the race.

Another guy who had been a huge supporter of my previous Death Valley mission was Jaron Mumby. He had organised my sponsorship and a lot of the marketing of the project for me. He's a national champion surf lifesaver and a real athlete, so he's really fit. He was keen for the adventure. He was a bit worried about crewing as he hadn't run long distances before, so I took him for a big run a few weeks before we left for Death Valley. We started from New Plymouth planning to do 70 kilometres, which is a bloody long way if you've specialised in sprinting and never run a marathon.

Jaron started off with me and I was running at my usual slow pace, plodding along. I could tell he really wanted to go a bit faster. He kept running ahead and dropping back. I just bided my time and when we got to about the 21-kilometre mark he was still going really strong. When we got to Okato, which is about 34 kilometres from New Plymouth, he started to fall behind and I was having to stop to wait for him. He didn't believe me when I told him I hadn't changed pace since the start. He reckoned I had sped up, but the truth was he hadn't managed to pace himself properly.

Jaron jumped in the crew car and I carried on around the coast. At about 55 kilometres, he decided to hop out and run the last few kilometres with me. Crewing is about getting in and out of the car and running with me, so I thought it would be good experience for him. He'd been in the car for a while and he found it really tough to get running again. I think it gave him a new understanding of what it is that I do.

With Jaron and Murray on board, I knew I needed some female energy and also a medic. The perfect combination of the two came along in the form of Megan Stewart. Megan is a paramedic and was introduced to me by a mutual friend of ours, Neil Wagstaff, who had crewed for me at Death Valley the year before.

As she tells the story, Megan was absolutely terrified when she first rang me because she wasn't a runner and wasn't sure she'd be able to help me out. I told her to come out for a run with me and see how we got on. She agreed but I knew she was a bit worried about what she was letting herself in for.

Our first run together was 35 kilometres up to the base of Mount Taranaki and back to New Plymouth. Megan was in a mild state of panic, so I told her I was really slow and I'd just cruise. Right from the start, we just got on so well. On that first run up the mountain there was a goat on the side of the road in the national park. Given it's a national park, the goat wasn't meant to be there. There was a ranger up the road so Megan told him about the goat. He obviously went and dealt with it because when we were running back down, the goat was in pieces. I was devastated. But goat or not, I knew this chick was the kind of person I wanted on my team.

That was the longest run that Megan had done by miles and she was really surprised she could do it. She tells me now that I distracted her by talking all the way and she didn't realise just how far she'd run.

Chris Cruikshank jumped onto the crew at the last minute. He'd been on the crew the previous year so he went from being a rookie to being the old hand on the team. He's always the big clown of the party and great fun—he keeps everyone laughing and was willing to do whatever was needed for the team.

Another key member of the crew was my friend Howard Dell. He's an amazing guy. Originally from Canada, he'd been a sponsor of mine in New Zealand but had got really sick and moved back to the United States. He had an incredible record as an athlete: he represented Canada in the bobsleigh at the 1988 Olympics, he played professional football in both Canada and the States, and he coached a heap of really successful track athletes.

The final member of the crew was Casey Potatau. I met first met Casey through champion boxer Shane Cameron, just as she was getting into running. At that stage she was keen to see how an ultra worked.

One of the things I learned from my previous effort at Badwater was that I needed more time to acclimatise to the temperatures in the desert than I'd thought, and also a little more time to get over jet lag. This time Megan and I headed over to the States two weeks before the race and met up with Gerhard, who'd flown in from Austria.

In the lead-up to the race, we stayed in a small town called Page in Arizona. We also took the chance to visit the Grand Canyon and Monument Valley. But mostly our time was spent training. The combination of the heat and altitude were a perfect testing ground for both me and Gerhard. The Arizona desert is absolutely beautiful but it was pretty hard going. Sometimes the wind would blow so hard, the sand felt like needles going into my skin—not the most comfortable of feelings.

The good thing about spending time in Arizona acclimatising was that when I went to meet the rest of my crew, I was feeling really good about racing in Death Valley. The fear I'd felt the previous year wasn't nearly as strong.

Getting back to Las Vegas from Arizona, Gerhard and I met up with the rest of our crews who had flown in from Austria and New Zealand respectively. There was only one man missing. Where was my old mate Howard Dell?

I was a bit worried that he hadn't turned up to meet us when he said he was going to. Of course, I didn't know what had happened to him until he emailed me a photo of himself lying in a hospital bed hooked up to all these machines. In his hand was a sign saying, 'Lisa, I'll be there somehow.'

I couldn't believe it. He was in Los Angeles and two days before he was due to travel he had a lung embolism and was admitted to hospital. At the time he was on the waiting list for a liver transplant and he was rushed into intensive care for treatment. But true to his word, he signed himself out of ICU at 10 p.m. that night and drove out to Death Valley because he didn't want to let me down.

The next morning we were having our briefing and he still hadn't turned up. I was really worried. It turned out that he'd arrived in at about 2 a.m. and gone to one of the crew rooms.

Unfortunately, the room he went to belonged to some of Gerhard's crew. They all freaked out to see this big black dude standing in their room in the middle of the night. They didn't know he was coming and that he was on my crew. They were scared out of their wits so they told him to get out.

The poor guy—he was deathly ill and ended up sleeping in his car in the heat of Death Valley. He finally found us after the briefing. We had to change all the crew names because we'd told the organisers Howard wasn't going to make it. I should have had more faith in him!

I felt a bit more comfortable about the race the second time round but you never feel really confident in an event like that. Knowing I was no longer a rookie was a good feeling, but Badwater is never something you can feel confident of finishing because there are so many things that can happen.

As it turned out, my second time at Death Valley was actually a harder race than the first. The pressure was on to improve my time so I went out with a different mindset. Instead of focusing on just finishing the race, I was thinking about my time and that's never good.

Instead of running by myself and setting my own pace, I decided to run with Gerhard. Even though I know he's faster than me, I planned to stay with him for the first 30 kilometres. Our strategy was for him to try to pull me along a little bit so I could improve on my time before he took off and ran his own race. I did that but the cost was huge. I ran 30 kilometres in 3 hours in heat that was mind-boggling—around the 55° Celsius mark. When we got to the first checkpoint at Furnace Creek Ranch, Gerhard motored off into the distance and I held back a wee bit. I really paid for that burst of speed dearly later on. Looking back, running at 10–11 kilometres an hour in the hottest part of Death Valley was a bit stupid.

After Gerhard left me, Murray Dick decided it was time for him to live his dream of running 10 kilometres with me in the desert. The poor guy really didn't know the sort of effect the heat would have. He jumped out of the crew car all keen to run. He started off OK but went downhill fast. He lasted 5 minutes before collapsing in a heap because of the heat and suffered all day from mild heat stroke.

When I arrived at Stovepipe Wells, the 70-kilometre mark, I was completely toasted. Even though I knew that I'd made it through the hottest part of the day and the hottest part of the valley, I also knew that out of Stovepipe Wells it's a 30-kilometre slog uphill that takes you 5000 feet up Townes Pass, the first of the two big passes in the race. And even though it's cooler than down in the valley, it's still over 40° up there at night.

On my way up Townes Pass, I started to have real trouble with my digestive system. I had acid build-up in my stomach from the gels that I'd been talked into using. They'd been fine in training but I'd had experience before that gels don't really work for me. I let myself be convinced that these ones were different and they'd be OK but I should have trusted my instinct and not taken them.

I started to vomit and pass out. My blood pressure was down around my ankles. I was 2 hours ahead of my previous year's schedule at that stage but I was not in good shape. I was so focused on beating my time that I almost blew the race. All night, I just kept fighting and fighting and I wouldn't take a break.

Looking back, I would have been better to take an hour off to rest and recover before getting back out there. Instead, I fought like a madwoman. I was passing out on the road and then getting up and wobbling along, barely even walking properly, let alone running.

I knew I still had so far to go and I didn't know how the

hell I was going to do it. All I knew was that I had to keep going. Sometimes determination can work against you. In that sort of situation, it's very hard to take a step back and go, 'Hang on, I'm probably going to lose an hour here but I can probably pick up my pace if I have a rest.' It's not always easy to make the right decisions on the spur of the moment or under that much pressure.

Getting up Townes Pass was an absolute mission. I don't really remember much about it— just that I kept passing out and falling over. I ran along holding onto Megan's arm and focused entirely on putting one foot in front of the other.

According to Megan, I kept saying to her, 'Tell me a story, tell me a story.' And off she went, 'Once upon a time, there was a runner called Lisa . . . ' Apparently she went through every story she could think of because I kept asking for more. I don't know if those stories were any good but they must have been interesting enough because I stayed on my feet and kept going. Well, most of the time.

Apparently, at one point, I was simultaneously crying and vomiting. Megan must have been wondering what the hell she'd got herself into out there in the desert with me being a big old mess. I was telling her I felt like shit and didn't know if I could go on. She was being all encouraging but then I did the one thing all crew members dread. I lay down in the middle of the road and absolutely refused to move.

I don't remember it at all, but Megan tells me she was cajoling me and nicely saying to me, 'Come on, Lisa, get up.' And I just yelled 'NO!' like a naughty kid. In that kind of situation it's really difficult for a crew member to know what to do. They're walking a really fine line—they don't want to give me a hard time but sometimes they need to be firm enough to get me restarted. It's tricky for them to know when to push and when to hold back. But Megan knew. Boy, did she know. She stopped, bent over me and yelled, 'FOR FUCK'S SAKE, GET UP OFF THE ROAD!'

Apparently, I started crying and said, 'Don't talk to me like that . . .' But then Megan gently picked me up off the road and we carried on up the pass.

From here, Megan takes up the story.

About 10 minutes later and she was even lower but she was still moving. It was dark so we were making our way by torchlight. I was looking around, keeping an eye on where we were going so she didn't stumble and fall over. Then I spotted this thing on the road just up ahead. It was like three cowpats stacked one on top of the other. They were huge. I thought I was seeing things. It was a very unlikely place to see cow shit.

Just as we got to it, I thought, 'Nope, those aren't cowpats.' So I grabbed Lisa around the waist, picked her up and made her jump over this thing. Then I turned around and looked back to see what it was. Only then did I realise that it was a Mojave green rattlesnake, which has the most toxic venom of all the rattlesnakes. I couldn't believe it. When I told people later that we'd run over a rattlesnake, they'd be like, 'Well, there's plenty of them squashed on the roads.' And I'd have to explain that we had actually run right over the top of a live rattlesnake.

I didn't know whether to tell Lisa or not. It could have freaked her out in the extreme or she might have gone 'Wow! How cool is that?', I wasn't sure. I decided to tell her. I said, 'Lis, Lis, we just ran over a snake!' She said, 'Did they?', thinking that I meant the guys in the support vehicle. 'No, we did, we did!'

All of this happened and I just kept on running. I had no idea what was going on. One minute I was running half asleep with Megan holding my arm. Then all of a sudden she picked me up and threw me over this thing in the road. I just carried on running, completely unmoved by all the drama.

Before long, it became clear to the crew that they had to do something about the fact that I had been unable to hold down any water or nutrition for a quite a while. I'm pretty sure me being in bad shape took Megan's mind off worrying about Howard. She was absolutely terrified that something was going to happen to him along the way, too. But Howard stuck by me the whole way and in the end he saved the race for me.

In the middle of the night I couldn't get any salts into me and my electrolytes were all out of kilter. Howard is such an experienced athlete that he could see what was happening. Because of his liver problems he'd been given a solution to help stabilise his own electrolytes. Howard got his solution of alkaline water and electrolytes and made me keep swishing it around inside my mouth. He wasn't trying to make me drink it because he knew I'd vomit it back up if I did. He just told me to put it in my mouth. It ended up that by doing this enough of the salts were absorbed by the membranes in my mouth to pull me back from the edge.

Howard would come out on the road and walk with me for a few minutes at a time. He'd sing me songs and tell me stories. He couldn't get out for very long or very often but he was always smiling. That meant so much to me. When it got tough, I'd think about what he was going through and the fact that he was still there supporting me. It really helped me keep putting one foot in front of the other. When other people fight so hard for me, the least I can do is not give up.

That was such a long night, but Megan stuck beside me and we were together right through it. I really struggled, constantly fighting the sleep demons and wanting to stop and lie down. Having got through the night and made it over Townes Pass, down through Panamint Valley and back up over Panamint Pass, I hit the long straight section of road that leads towards Lone Pine. That piece of road is a mind-blowing 50-kilometre long straight that never seems to end.

While I was running along that straight, early the next morning, I could hear this really loud noise. It was a couple of military jets on manoeuvres from the nearby air force base. They came so low it felt like they were just a few feet above us. The good thing is that I could feel everything in my body reverberate as they flew over me.

As they went over, Megan started yelling, 'Jets! Jets! Jets!' It was like the very sight of them supercharged both of us with a rush of adrenaline that kickstarted my body. They kept coming back and swooping over us. I remember Megan asking me what I thought the pilot looked like. It seemed like a bit of a dumb question at the time but I thought about it for a minute, then turned round and said, 'A pilot.'

After the planes, I started slowly coming right. It's amazing how you can be in such a perilous state and still come back from it. It's not over until you lie down and say it's over. If you take a rest at the right time, it can make all the difference.

Despite his disastrous running effort the previous day, Murray wasn't put off trying to achieve what he'd come out here to do. He was absolutely determined to go back to New Plymouth saying he'd run 10 kilometres of Death Valley with me. And anyone who knows Murray won't be surprised that he managed it with ease. The guy is an absolute Taranaki legend.

The next major milestone along the road for me was the 100-mile mark, which is at 161 kilometres. It is in the middle of that 50-kilometre straight—a horrible part of the run. When you're running for that distance on an almost dead straight piece of road you feel like you're running on a treadmill. The vista doesn't change, and you feel like you're going nowhere. In an effort to give me a boost on this massive straight, the crew worked out exactly where the 100-mile mark was. Then they all got out of the cars and were dancing and singing in the middle of the road. I was running along thinking, What the hell are they doing?

When I got to them they were all congratulating me for doing 100 miles. I thought, Great, only 35 miles more to go—that's 56 kilometres. It was a huge boost. But then, a couple of kilometres down the road, they realised they'd miscalculated. They had to come out and tell me that it hadn't been the 100-mile point back there and that I had only just passed it. That might seem like a really small thing but it almost wrecked me mentally. It was a real downer as I'd calculated how far I had left to go and it felt like they'd added a couple of miles to the race. It's not as bad as getting lost, but it's enough to make you swear at your crew.

The last 20 kilometres of the race climb 8000 feet up Mount Whitney to the finish line at Whitney Portal. I got to the bottom of Mount Whitney late on the second day. Heading up the hill, I had no idea that my race was close to being wrecked by something I had no control over.

Half the mountain was on fire. It had been so hot that bushfires had spontaneously broken out on the part of the mountain we were meant to be running on. There's me trying to run up the road and there are police cars and fire engines racing past us. All I could think was 'The finish line is up there'. As I was slowly winding my way up the mountain there was smoke everywhere—fantastic for my asthmatic little lungs.

The next thing we knew there was a police car pulling in next to us and a policeman shouting at us, 'Everyone off the mountain! We're evacuating the whole area. The race is over!' My crew just told me to keep going—that's how determined we all were. None of us cared that it was a cop telling us to leave. There was no way anyone was going to tell us my race was finished. I'd spent two days trying to run here and I was bloody well going to make it to the end whether they liked it or not. I wasn't leaving that mountain until the race director himself told me the race was over. I just kept going onwards and upwards. Nothing was going to stop me. Not a fire, not an American cop—nothing and nobody.

Some of the other runners behind me listened to the cop. They stopped and, apparently, they were left sitting on the side of the road completely inconsolable. Unbeknownst to us, the race director was having nightmares up the top. They had to evacuate the finish line but they got permission to move it 2 kilometres down the road. So, for that year, Badwater Ultramarathon was slightly shorter than previous races.

Luckily, by keeping going I got to finish the race even more quickly than I thought I would. I wasn't expecting the finish line to be where it was—I thought I had further to go and suddenly there it was. I went over the finish line going, 'Is that it? Am I really done?' I couldn't believe it. Instead of bawling my eyes out like I had the year before, I was absolutely stoked. I'd held my reserves in for another couple of kilometres, which is another 40 minutes or so. I crossed the line at 11.15 p.m., having taken 37 hours 15 minutes to complete the race. Despite all my troubles, I'd improved on my previous time by 1 hour and 10 minutes, and improved two places from tenth to eighth. I was stoked.

Although my race was over, there was a drama unfolding on the other side of the world. With all the trouble caused by the fire and some runners finishing at the old finish line, some at the new finish line and some not finishing because of the evacuation, the race organisers had so much on their plate they stopped updating the times on the internet. My parents were watching the live feed on the web back in New Plymouth. They also knew there was a forest fire on Mount Whitney and they knew I was in the general vicinity. When they didn't see me finish long after they thought I should have, they both started to get really worried. Their concern was finally relieved when I made a quick phone call to let them know I was finished and that I was fine.

As for Gerhard, who I'd last seen leaving Furnace Creek all those miles ago? Well, I'd been hearing he was doing really well throughout the race. He was right there with the race leaders all the way to the 200-kilometre mark but he had pushed it too hard in the early stages. He hit the wall and the last 17 kilometres took him 5 hours, which is crawling pace. He finished the race in ninth, which is still bloody good, but it just proves that pacing yourself, no matter how experienced you are, is vital.

Lisa's advice on getting started

I didn't really set out to coach. I just seem to have an influence on the people around me. Some people start crewing for me and end up running further than they ever thought possible. It's a bit like being a drug pusher—except I'm an ultramarathon pusher. People around me seem to end up running or doing ultras whether they like it or not.

I really enjoy working with women. I find it easier to train with women than men. It's probably because men tend to be quite fast over a short distance and it's a bit harder to coach them into running with the longer race in mind. If someone wants to be super-fast, then I'm the wrong person to be working with them. I'm never going to be a marathon runner or be able to train a marathon runner, but if you want to go long I can help.

If you want to give it a go—do. Take that first step and keep taking those steps. And don't give up the first time you fail. For my very first running experience, I signed up for a 10-kilometre fun run when I was in my early twenties. I had an asthma attack and had to pull out after 5 kilometres. If I'd taken that as a big failure and a sign to not go on with running, that would have been such a waste. What I learned was that I went out too fast and that short races aren't for me. I'll struggle over 10 kilometres and come in towards the back of the pack. Over 200 kilometres I'll still struggle, but I'll beat most of the other runners.

Don't put any expectations on yourself in terms of times. Forget the clock. That's the biggest thing that I've seen half-marathoners and marathoners do. They feel like they have to beat the 2-hour or the 4-hour barrier. That's rubbish. Just do the damn thing. Don't worry about your time—run the distance in however long it takes you.

Another thing a lot of people think is that after one race, the next time they race that distance they have to improve their time. It doesn't always work like that so don't get despondent. I might run a marathon in 3 hours 45 minutes and the next one might take me 4 hours and 30 minutes. You can't always better your time because conditions change, your body changes and the course changes.

If you're going to go for times then ultramarathon running probably isn't for you. For most of us, it's about getting to the finish line in whatever way, shape or form we can. You never know what a race route is going to throw at you. You don't know what the temperatures are going to be, you don't know what the wind is going to be like, you don't know what physical ailments you're likely to encounter. What will get you there is the attitude that you're just going to keep taking the next step. If you are a beginner and you think 'I can't run 5 kilometres, that's too far', get out of your head that it's a 5-kilometre course. Just go out there to have some fun. Don't put that pressure on yourself, just enjoy the experience without any expectations.

If you're going to run with other people, run with someone who runs at the same speed as you. If you're slowing down to their pace, you'll find it frustrating. If you have to speed up to keep up, you'll end up overdoing it.

I've trained a lot of people from zero and it's getting people through the first three months that's most difficult because most people's brains aren't hardwired to have exercise every day. But sticking with it and exercising every day, after three months your brain will be reprogrammed to expect you to get out and exercise every day. After that, it's much easier to make the time and find the motivation to go for a run or walk.

Those first three months are horrible. You'll probably see

very little in the way of results and you'll wonder why the hell you are bothering. You'll get tired and you'll get sick of it and you might lose your motivation. Just remember that it will get easier at the end of those three months. While you're establishing that routine, it's really important to be kind to yourself. Don't look at the scales, don't worry about your times, don't focus on running a marathon. Just focus on establishing a regular fitness routine. Commit to exercising every day regardless of what the outcome is over that first three months. That's all.

2
Representing New Zealand

If in doubt, go running. Solutions to problems come to you. It clarifies your mind. It's a meditation of sorts.

Commonwealth Mountain and Ultra Distance Running Championships, 17–18/9/2009

After getting home from Death Valley, I had just over two months to recover and train for the Commonwealth Ultra Distance Running Championships. I know it goes against every piece of advice I ever give about making sure your body has plenty of time to recover between events, but there was absolutely no way that I was going to miss out on my first chance to represent my country. Besides, I'd worked bloody hard to qualify for those champs. Death Valley or no Death Valley, I was going to be on that plane to England in September if it killed me.

The qualifying race for the Commonwealth champs was

the Sri Chinmoy Self Transcendence 24-hour track race, which also serves as the New Zealand 24-hour national championships. In 2008 it was held at the Millennium Stadium in Auckland and there were 31 of us running in the 6-, 12- and 24-hour races.

Lining up alongside me at the start of the race was my old mate Mad Macca, or Staff Sergeant Alex McKenzie as he's known to his army colleagues. Me and Macca have run several ultra-races together and whenever we do, we'll always have each other's backs. We both had Commonwealth qualification distances in our sights at the nationals. I had to do 185 kilometres and Macca needed to knock off 200 kilometres—all of which had to be done going around and around the 400-metre running track at the stadium.

I felt pretty good throughout the race. I did the first 100 kilometres in a personal best time of 11 hours 26 minutes and I knew I was on track to make the required 185-kilometre mark. In fact, I made the Commonwealth qualifying mark with plenty of time to spare.

Macca, on the other hand, had it a bit tougher. After 22 hours 30 minutes he had run 189 kilometres. The chances of him getting to the magic 200-kilometre mark must have seemed pretty slim to the other people watching him but I knew my mate could make it—even though he didn't seem so sure himself. I got alongside him and gave him a really good rev up. I told him that he was out there representing the New Zealand army and that he had to do his soldiers proud. I told him that there was no way he was going to give up and that he just had to dig it in.

Something must have got through to him because the shutters went down and he just took off. For a man who had been running since nine the previous morning, he could really move. His lap time went from an average of 3 minutes 30 seconds per lap down to 2 minutes 10 seconds. He was absolutely motoring and there was no way I could keep up with him—he lapped me, then lapped me, then lapped me again. Whatever pain he'd been in just moments before wasn't even registering in his brain. Macca was determined to give it everything he had, even though he wasn't sure he'd make the cut. It just shows the spirit and the commitment of the guy—he appeared to have nothing left in the tank yet he still managed to make the 200-kilometre mark with just 8 minutes to go.

Once he'd made the 200 kilometres, he collapsed in a heap. This time there really was nothing left in him. The officials were telling him to get up and keep going just in case they'd miscalculated the distance. He'd used up every last bit of energy and just standing up was an absolute mission for the poor bugger. It's moments like that which I love about our sport. There's nothing quite like seeing an athlete who thinks they have absolutely nothing left just pull out that last bit of energy to reach their goal.

Macca and I were pretty happy campers on the podium that day. He'd won the men's title and I got the women's title. Macca's final distance was 200.9 kilometres and I did 192.3—a personal best. We were both going to England to represent New Zealand the following year. We were stoked.

Making the qualifying times also meant that Macca and I had qualified for the 2009 World Championships, being held in Italy. Unfortunately, Athletics New Zealand decided not to send a team in 2009 because the 2008 Olympics had swallowed up all their funds. Eventually they gave us permission to compete as individuals representing New Zealand but we didn't find out until the day entries closed. As much as I would have loved to have run at the world champs, there was no way I could come up with the $10,000 it would cost that quickly. Still, the Commonwealth champs was a great achievement.

The organisers of the Commonwealth championships are trying to get the 24-hour event and the 100-kilometre event considered for the Commonwealth Games program. I reckon it would be awesome for the sport to be given that kind of status as it would be an acknowledgement of all the thousands of athletes who participate in long-distance events every year. First stop, the Commonwealth Games . . . roll on the Olympics.

At the age of 40 I never thought I'd be able to finally achieve my dream of representing New Zealand. I'd always wanted to be in a national team and I finally got there. It just goes to show that if you have a dream you should never give up on it. While I was stoked about pulling on New Zealand colours, I think my dad, Cyril, was even more proud. He reckons all he ever wanted was for one of his kids to represent New Zealand at something!

One of the great things about representing New Zealand was that, for once, I got to be part of a team. Alongside me and Macca in the 24-hour team were Val Muskett from Waikouaiti, and Vivian Cheng from Wellington. The 24-hour champs were being held in conjunction with the Commonwealth Mountain Running Championships so the four of us joined a team of ten Kiwi mountain runners headed for England. It was a total buzz for me to be in a national team alongside an athlete of the calibre of world champion mountain runner Melissa Moon.

So there I was, not that long back from Death Valley, getting on another plane for another flight to the other side of the world. It's not just the racing that can really mess up your body when you're an ultrarunner. Living in New Zealand, it's a sad fact that most of the races I do require me to take long-haul flights. And with the long-haul flights usually comes the dreaded jet lag. I always try to spend at least a week in a location before race day but sometimes that just isn't possible. Arriving in England, I only had a few days before the race and I did my best to conquer the 12-hour time difference.

The race was going to be held in a town called Keswick, in the Lake District. It is an absolutely gorgeous setting. The town is right on the edge of Derwentwater and the surrounding hills—or fells, as the locals call them—were the ideal spot for a bit of training and for getting out in the sun to try to shake off the jet lag.

The whole 24-hour team and crew stayed in one house. It was a great way for us all to bond. Alongside the four of us were my mum, Isobel, Val's husband, John, and Vivian's husband, Richard.

In the morning, before the start of the 24-hour race, there was a fantastic opening ceremony with all the athletes from the fourteen competing nations parading with their national flags. From there, we all headed over to Fitz Park in Keswick, where we would be competing. Instead of having a 400-metre track, the park had a 1-kilometre loop on footpaths around the park.

Macca hadn't been going so well in the lead-up to the race. He'd mentioned a couple of times that he had a bit of pain in one of his shins. Given that's pretty normal for most ultra-runners we didn't think too much of it at the time. He had a check-up and reckoned he'd be fine. Having absolutely busted his arse to qualify for the race, taken time off from the army, and paid a fortune to get to Keswick, there was nothing and no-one that was going to stop Macca from running his race. Well, almost nothing.

The race started in fine weather and there we all were proudly decked out in our black running uniforms. There's nothing that quite compares to the feeling of wearing black with the silver fern to represent your country.

About an hour and a half into the race, I turned around and saw Macca limping along. Given how hardcore he is, I knew it wasn't good. I carried on running but I could tell whatever was wrong with him was getting worse.

An hour later and seventeen laps into the race, Macca was pulled off the track by officials who called for a medic to check him out. In a 24-hour race like this, your aim is to run around it as often as you can in the time allocated. This meant that I had to keep any stops to an absolute mini-mum—there was no way I could stop to find out what was happening with my mate.

I was lucky that Marion, one of my friends from when I was living in Austria, had come over to support me. She managed to get alongside me and tell me that Macca's leg was broken. I couldn't believe it. Apparently, he'd had a stress fracture in his shin—probably from some of the hard-out army training he was involved with just before he left New Zealand—and his leg had broken right through. Typical Macca. Even with a broken leg, he'd tried to run through the pain. It took every-thing the officials had to convince Macca his race was over. He was absolutely gutted and I was gutted for him. Mum did the best she could to comfort him but even my amazing mum couldn't do anything that would make him feel any better. All the hard work he'd done on that Auckland track all those months before, all the money, time and training, and there he was on the sideline with a broken leg. Macca's race was over. For an ultrarunner, it doesn't get much worse than that.

While I was worried about what was going on for my mate, I couldn't afford to let it affect my race. I had to carry on. but I wasn't having a good day either. Even after spending a few days acclimatising, I was still struggling with jet lag and I hadn't been able to get my sleep patterns sorted. The race started at midday and by late afternoon I was already starting to nod off as I ran. It was clear that it was going to be a long night for me. I knew that as it got darker and colder, things were only going to get worse.

As soon as evening fell, I was fighting the sleep monsters big time—they are horrible things. My body was just so fatigued and my body clock was completely out of whack from travelling, I just kept nodding off while I was still running. I knew I had to keep going but the colder it got, the more I wanted to sleep, and boy did it get cold in Keswick.

There's not much you can do to fight the sleep monsters. It's a mind battle. You can't take caffeine tablets because they produce acid and upset your digestion. I always try to keep more sugar coming in to keep me awake, but it's really just a mental battle to stop sleeping.

Because we were running in a park rather than on a purpose-built athletics track, the path didn't have permanent floodlighting. The organisers got four huge floodlights installed temporarily. Unfortunately, these weren't set up as well as they could have been. One of them shone right into our eyes as we came into the feeding station but didn't really light the track very well. That wasn't the worst of it, though. The two lights at the back of the track were so tall that they were above the treetops. This meant that the light had to filter through the tree canopy and all we got was a kind of dappled light and a lot of shadows.

It was down this poorly lit back stretch of the trail that I really struggled. Whenever I got into the dark, my body just wanted to go to sleep. I'd keep running but fall asleep and only wake up if I veered off the course into a tree or if I'd fallen over—it's not an ideal way to be running when all you want to do is cover heaps of distance.

Out in the darkest corner, there was an English bloke who was supporting one of his own runners. He obviously knew how hard the darkness was for us and chose the worst spot on the track to support from, which was pretty cool. At one point he yelled out to me, 'Hey, why are you always going to sleep on this corner?' I said, 'Mate, I'm going to sleep all the way round!' He said, 'Every time you come around here you're wobbling everywhere.'

The next time I came around he goes, 'Hey, your name's Tamati, eh?' I'm like, 'Ummm yeah.' Then he calls out, 'Are you any relation to Howie?' I couldn't believe it! He'd been coached by my second cousin Howie when he was over in England coaching league. It just proves that I can't get away from my family anywhere, no matter how far I run! It was hilarious and lifted my spirits.

Running a race like this, the role of my crew and supporters is vital. There's no way I could have finished the Commonwealth champs without my mum and Marion. The pair of them stayed out all night in the freezing cold to help keep me moving. I'm pretty sure that they would rather have been in their warm beds than out in the cold Lake District night and their dedication meant everything to me.

In a 24-hour race, you can't stop—you have to keep fighting. To be competitive, you've got to be out there for 23 hours and 50 minutes and the rest is toilet stops. If you need any more downtime than that you're not going to make it. I fought the sleep monster all night and it only came right when the sun came up just as the race was about to finish.

Val Muskett—who was 55 at the time and is a total inspiration to me—finished in fifth place having covered a massive

201.4 kilometres. Vivien Cheng made it over the line in ninth place with 191.7 kilometres.

Me, well, it wasn't my day. Qualifying for the champs I had run my personal best of 193.2 kilometres, but in the actual race I only managed to make 163 kilometres, which was really disappointing. I came in nineteenth out of twenty-two runners. At least I'd finished the race and represented my country.

Ultimately, I was disappointed by the distance I ran but I knew that my body hadn't fully recovered from Death Valley. Even though I felt OK physically, my core strength and resilience weren't there. I tend to think I'm bulletproof and that I can do ten races a year. It's just not true. When something like Death Valley comes along it takes far more out of your body than you realise. From the reading I've done, it can take six to twelve months before your body is fully recovered. So to turn around and do a 24-hour race so soon after a race like that was really stupid.

I had been hoping to do 190–200 kilometres but that just wasn't going to happen—there was no way. Things like adrenal exhaustion just can't be fixed. In a race like Death Valley, your body uses up a lot of cortisol and electrolytes that can't be regenerated quickly. Even though you might feel OK on a day-to-day basis, you haven't got that depth of strength needed to pull out a really good performance.

Getting older I'm starting to feel the limitations of my body and trying to be more reasonable. I used to do as many races as I could fit in, but now I have to be more careful about how many races I commit to. Now I take a bit more stock of what I'm doing and I try to peak at the right time for each race. For me, doing major events twice a year is about right; by a major event I mean 100 miles upwards. But in order to do two in a calendar year, they have to be a few months apart. Outside of those, I can do a few more minor events, but I know that I'm not going to be super competitive in those.

And what of my mate Macca? Well, Mum and I flew home with him and his uncast broken leg. When he got back to New Zealand the break was reassessed and he had to spend three months in a moon boot. But that wasn't going to stop him. When I decided on my next mad challenge, Macca was one of the first to volunteer to join me.

Oh, and just in case you're wondering, Macca went back to the 2011 Commonwealth championships in Wales. He finished eighth, running a massive 217 kilometres in 24 hours.

Finding the perfect shoe

Being on my feet a lot, good running shoes are absolutely vital to me. As every person has different feet and a different running style there are absolutely no one-size-fits-all solutions to the question 'Which running shoes should I buy?'. Buying new running shoes can be an absolute minefield at the best of times. Add the trend for barefoot running to the mix and there often seems to be more questions than answers.

Rajat Chauhan is an ultrarunner and a doctor specialising in musculoskeletal medicine and sports and exercise medicine. In 2010 he founded the world's highest altitude ultra-race—La Ultra The High—a gruelling 222-kilometre ultramarathon that crosses two passes high in the Himalayan mountains. Here is his advice on buying new shoes.

Can your shoes make you a better athlete?

It's commonly assumed that good shoes make a better athlete. Surprisingly, there is no evidence of this. Australian researcher (also a runner and physician) Craig Richards and his team noted in a 2008 *British Journal of Sports Medicine* article:

> Since the 1980s, distance running shoes with thick, heavily cushioned heels and features to control how much the heel rolls in, have been consistently recommended to runners who want to avoid injury. We did not identify a single study that has attempted to measure the effect of this shoe type on either injury rates or performance.

Dr Richards took note of Dutch research that found that 37–56 per cent of recreational runners are injured at least once a year, mainly in the leg or foot. The standard shoe recommendation doesn't seem to work. Indeed, given the lack of research, we can't make any evidence-based shoe recommendations.

At Harvard University, professor of biological anthropology Daniel Lieberman's current projects include 'How humans run barefoot (and why it may be good for you)'. Dr Lieberman was quoted in the *Daily Mail* in May as saying, 'Until 1972, when the modern athletic shoe was invented, people ran in very thin-soled shoes, had strong feet and had a much lower incidence of knee injuries.'

What price a perfect fit?

A study published in the *British Journal of Sports Medicine* in 2008 showed that 'cheap and moderately priced running shoes are just as good, if not better than, more expensive ones in terms of cushioning impact and overall comfort.' It also pointed out that 'comfort is a subjective sensation based on individual preferences and is not related to cost or cushioning'. Interestingly, a 1989 study by Bernard Marti (a leading preventive medicine specialist from Switzerland) showed that 'runners wearing top-of-the-line running shoes were 123% more likely to get injured than runners in cheaper running shoes'.

So, you can't count on cost guaranteeing quality.

Should you go by gait?

You should know your gait, but going only by that yardstick is like getting married solely on the basis of horoscope matching. Sometimes, gait analysis can be a completely useless exercise.

Shun brand loyalty

It happens even to experienced runners. By the time they figure out which particular shoe from a particular brand works for them, the shoe company introduces a new and improved version. Surprisingly, this doesn't suit, so it's back to the shops.

Does size matter?

There is often no standardisation, even within the same company. At times, even the same-size same-model measurements can differ between pairs. Ordering through friends abroad, because online prices in the US, for instance, can be much cheaper, is a bad idea. Never buy without trying.

Don't run in the 'right' size

Formal shoes must fit you perfectly, but running shoes must be half a size or one size bigger. There needs to be at least a finger-width gap between your longest toe and the end of the shoe. Width is crucial, too. Your feet need space to breathe and to swell. It should feel as if you are not wearing anything.

Should you rotate your runners?

It's a great idea to have two pairs and keep rotating them— and let one pair have 200 kilometres less on it, so you don't wear both out at once. But stick to the same model.

When should you replace your shoes?

You need to say goodbye after 500–800 kilometres of running together, which means keeping a log. More important, though, is whether you land heavily or lightly on your feet. Check the soles—if they are worn flat, it's time they were replaced. Also, a shoe that has run just 200 kilometres but has been sitting for two years is not 'young'. Rubber loses cushioning properties as it ages. Use shoes for 1 year, max, and then shop for a new pair.

What to look for

Running shoes must be very flexible to put your feet in control.

There's no point having extra weights tied to your legs—almost all running shoes now are reasonably lightweight.

Don't fuss about looks. I suggest that you go with the adage 'if they feel good, they look good'.

Is barefoot running for you?

Here Rajat shares his thoughts on the barefoot running phenomenon that is gaining popularity.

•

British physician Mike Stroud in his book *Survival of the Fittest: Understanding Health and Peak Performance* suggested that humans are best suited for a hot, not cold, climate. Had some of our ancestors not decided to move to colder climates, we may never have had footwear. Yet most of us can hardly conceive of athletes running a race without 'proper' shoes.

It's a while since South African running sensation and Olympian Zola Budd trained and ran barefoot, but in recent years going barefoot, both for races and regular fitness runs, is finding more adherents in developed countries.

Erik Trinkaus, professor of physical anthropology at Washington University, St Louis, suggested that the first supportive footwear appeared 26,000–30,000 years ago (*Journal of Archaeological Science*, July 2005). Analysing anatomical evidence from early modern humans and their Upper Palaeolithic ancestors, he said, 'The bones of the little toes of humans from that time frame were much less strongly built than those of their ancestors, while their leg bones remained large and strong.' He suggested the most likely cause for this was the introduction of supportive footwear.

A quarter of the bones in the body are in the feet—there are 26 on each side. Each foot has 33 joints each and there are more than 100 muscles, ligaments and tendons aside. There are 250,000 sweat glands in each foot to cool them, which are made redundant when you wears shoes. There are more nerve endings on your soles than any other part of your body, suggesting that touching and feeling the ground is important. The foot can sustain enormous pressure—several tonnes over the course of a 1-mile run—with in-built flexibility and resiliency. The ankle serves as a foundation, shock absorber and propulsion engine, so do we need shoes at all? Or were we designed to run barefoot?

No-shoes shoes

Is the shoe industry ignoring the facts? Not really. Research and development departments at leading footwear companies have a new goal—a running shoe that recreates the barefoot environment. It's a good compromise. Called minimalist shoes, these include the startling Vibram FiveFingers and also mainstream brands such as Nike Free or Teva Proton series. There's also the traditional Mexican *huarache* sandal.

Should you shed your shoes for good?

Despite all I have said, I would find that extreme. Even if we agree that shoes are making our feet weaker, our feet are simply not accustomed to going bare any more. When a cast is put over a limb for 4–6 months, the muscles atrophy by 40–60 per cent, and here we are talking about giving up after 20–40 years of wearing shoes for more than 12 hours a day.

If you are keen, change very gradually—first, just walk

barefoot around the house, then walk on your lawn or a sandy beach for a few minutes a day, and so on. Honestly, it doesn't seem very practical out on the road, given hygiene and safety issues. It's more realistic to wear shoes, however basic, for their original protective purpose.

Lisa's advice on post-race recovery

Endurance-wise and experience-wise I'm as strong as I ever was, but I can't achieve the post-race speedy recovery that I used to.

Recovery from an ultramarathon can take a long time. Some experts suggest that full recovery can take up to 6 months after a short ultra and up to 12 months after a really long hard-out race. Many ultramarathoners I know compete far more frequently than that, but I have noticed that their careers tend to be shorter than runners who compete less frequently.

I have experienced extreme burn-out after trying to compete in too many races within a year. In 2009, for example, I ran in a 100-kilometre event, the Badwater Ultra at Death Valley, the 24-hour Commonwealth championships and the 2250-kilometre Run Through New Zealand. By the end of the year, I was mentally and physically totalled. It took me a really long time to recover and, if I am honest, I don't think I've ever rebuilt the strength and resilience I had before those races. So if you want to do as I say and not as I do, here's my advice on how best to recover after running a long race.

Your body is likely to be in overdrive so you might feel fine for a while, but what I've noticed is that I've usually got a high going on. I might be in pain from all the delayed onset muscle soreness and all the rest of it but I'll be buzzing from completing the race.

You will be on an adrenaline high but your body won't sustain that. I find that often about 10 days after an event, I'll crash mentally and physically. It's because I've used up all my stress hormones, and my endorphins will be at an all-time low. It can take at least 6 weeks for your bloods to return to normal and to rebuild. On a cellular level it takes even longer.

All of those depletions start to come through and it affects my sleep. When that crash comes, you really need to be taking it easy on yourself—that means for the couple of weeks following a race. It's not uncommon to get depressed in that phase, too. It's usually because you've completed a huge task that you've been training hard out for and you've been focused on for a really long time. Once you've achieved that goal, you might feel like you've lost your focus. It's a good time to take stock and know that your body is recovering. Give it time to do that.

If you're an addicted athlete, you can get back running pretty soon. If possible, though, in those first two weeks after a big race try to do non-impact training. Don't push yourself too hard and focus on recovery. Easy, slow bike-riding or swimming will keep your muscles moving while giving your joints time to recover. Anything where you're not completely weight bearing is good.

Rest, nutrition and giving your body time to recover are really important. When you're young your body rebuilds faster, but as you get older you'll need more time. I've seen athletes who can do one massive mission after another but invariably after three or four years of going full out they crash. Going like that will shorten your career span heaps and that's not ideal. As a runner at a top level, your career span is about twenty years from when you start, but you can bust your guts so much that your running career span may be shortened.

3
The length of the country

While I'm racing, my mind is constantly preoccupied with taking the next step.

The NZ Run, 31/10 – 14/12/2009

When I was younger, I always wanted to run the length of New Zealand. It's always been on my bucket list. Coming back home from Death Valley the first time, I needed a new project to focus on. It's inevitable that when you complete a big race like that, you struggle with not having a big goal to aim for anymore.

Looking around for a new project, the idea of running the length of my home country just kept coming back to me. I knew that I was never going to shake the idea unless I got out and did the run, so I decided that if I was going to do it I'd do it for charity. And so the NZ Run project was born. I've had so much amazing support from people over the years that I really wanted to be able to put something back into the community that has looked after me so well.

My mate Macca's nephew had been struggling with cancer for years and Macca had done some fundraising stuff for CanTeen. They're a charity that works to support young people living with cancer. They not only support kids with cancer but also their siblings and families. They were an obvious choice for me to run for. They were really supportive and excited about what I was planning to do. I am still an ambassador for them and have been privileged to design bandanas for them for the past few years.

Given how big the project was, I decided it would be good to have more than one charity to work for. That's when Cure Kids came on board. They provide funding for research into life-threatening childhood illnesses in New Zealand. Over the years, this research has helped save many young lives and improved the quality of life for thousands of children. I've worked with them ever since and they're now the official charity of my Northburn 100 race.

Another part of my mission was to involve schools in what I was doing by setting my 'K Per Day Challenge'. Through the challenge, I encouraged schoolkids along the way to choose something active—biking, walking, running, kayaking, canoeing, surfing, whatever they were into—and set themselves a time or distance goal, committing to the goal for a minimum period of two weeks. For example, they might commit to run 5 kilometres a day for 14 days or walk 1 kilometre every day for a month. It didn't really matter what the goal was so long as it meant they'd get outside and get active.

I then challenged the kids to get sponsorship from family and friends to be paid when they achieved their goal. It was a great way to fundraise for my charities and help kids learn life skills that would help them stay healthy at the same time. To really reinforce the project, I planned to visit schools where kids had taken up the challenge as I made my way through the country..

It was a massive undertaking that took almost a year to organise—I had no idea how big the project would become. It was the first time I'd taken on anything quite so big. There was a whole team of us pulling it together but even then it was almost too big for us.

One of the first things I had to get sorted was sponsorship. Luckily, my old mate Murray Dick hadn't been put off the whole ultrarunning gig after his experience in the super-heat of Death Valley. Murray's commitment and dedication to this project were there from the outset and, with him and the team from Taranaki Engineering on board as naming rights' sponsor, I knew that the project was going to not only get off the ground but that it would fly.

Another one of my Death Valley team, Jaron Mumby from Fire Design, got right behind the Run Through New Zealand. Jaron not only took on the task of providing creative media solutions for the project, he also quickly had a website up and running before turning his skills to designing promotional material for the run. And as if all that wasn't enough, Jaron also took on the role of project manager for the whole shebang.

David Casey at Big Media was another great sponsor who also ended up on the crew for the run. He did heaps of promotional work to make sure that as many people as possible knew I was running and why.

It's when I'm pulling together a big project like this that I'm really grateful to live in a place like New Plymouth. Before long we had a couple of brand-new Toyota Prius cars for the crew to do the trip in courtesy of Kevin and James at Tasman Toyota. Taranaki Steelformers also got behind the project and provided us with much-needed funding. Other local companies who got in behind me were The Frontrunner, More FM, Mobilize and Waitara Travel.

But it wasn't just local companies who saw the benefit of what I was attempting to do. Maui Campervans gave us one of their vans to use as a support vehicle throughout the country. It was a huge help and Pams donated a whole lot of food for the duration of the trip, which was all packed into the campervan.

One of the tricky things about doing a trip like this in New Zealand is that little bit of water between the islands called Cook Strait. Interislander ferries sponsored the passage for all of the crew and our support vehicles, which was a massive help. So between all of them, and other sponsors Bartercard, Nature Spring Water and Buff, we knew we had what we needed to make this run a reality.

With the money to do the trip secured, putting together a champion crew was the next big thing on the agenda. This was the first event I'd ever done in New Zealand and it was fantastic to be able to have my family on board. My amazing mum, Isobel, has always been my biggest supporter so she quickly signed on for the duration of the run. I don't think she's ever had so many days off work in a row and, even though she knew it was going to be tough, I suspect she was quite looking forward to having a bit of a holiday along the way. My dad, Cyril, and my brother, Mitch, also joined the crew and were happy to come and run with me some of the way.

My cousin Eileen was also a key part of the crew—she had the huge job of arranging accommodation for everyone along the way. Even though we had the campervan, heaps of motels and hotels throughout the country provided us with very welcome and comfortable beds to sleep in each night and much of that was down to Eileen's hard work.

I had a friend come over from the States, Jason Obirek. I met him at Death Valley and told him my plans. He offered to come over and run with me, which was great. He's a great trainer and has crewed for loads of ultrarunners so he had a fair idea of the sort of rehab I'd be needing at the end of each day. I don't think he really knew what he was getting himself in for with all of us Kiwis, but I assured him that, whatever happened, it would definitely be an adventure.

Even though he was still in a moonboot from his exploits at the Commonwealth champs, there was no way my mate Macca was going to miss out on the excitement of a project like this— he promised to join me for as much of the run as he could.

The two final pieces of the crew puzzle are my two best mates, Megan Stewart, who had been such an amazing asset in Death Valley, and Nadene George.

If it hadn't been for the NZ Run, I might never have met Nadene. She and my cousin Eileen are friends. Eileen knew she did a bit of running so rang and asked her if she wanted to come and crew for me. We met briefly at a book signing and she agreed to join me for a couple of weeks. It speaks volumes for the kind of person she is that she put everything on hold to come and support a runner she barely knew.

This time, it wasn't just Megan's paramedical skills I called on for the project. She's an incredibly organised and focused person and she took charge of all the pre-planning—she dotted every 'i' and crossed every 't'. She made sure all our insurance was sorted out, she sussed out traffic management and plotted the best route for me to run. Without her, we'd have been in all sorts of trouble.

With sponsors, crew and logistics all sorted, there was

now only one thing for it. I had to run the length of New Zealand from Bluff in the south to Cape Reinga in the north. How hard could it be? It's only 2200 kilometres and would take me 33 days. That's an average of 66.6 kilometres a day, give or take. Oh gosh, me and my big mouth had gone and done it again and I was really going to have to do this now.

So, early on the morning of 31 October, I found myself in Bluff with Mum, Mitch, Murray, Jaron and Jason. The chairman of the Bluff Oyster Festival, John Edminstin, was there to see us on our way and after a few photos with the crew and a 10-second countdown, the NZ Run was officially underway. It was an emotional moment for me. A year of planning and organising was finally coming to fruition and I was thrilled about that. But I was also a little scared of the mammoth task ahead of me. That fear was soothed a bit by having Murray Dick running alongside me for the first few kilometres. Murray's belief in me has never faltered so I couldn't think of anyone better to have beside me at the start of day one.

It was pretty cold and I found it difficult to get comfortable over the first 30 kilometres between Bluff and Invercargill. As the day warmed up, though, I started to hit my stride and feel good. Jaron ran with me for about 3 hours that day and it was a good chance for us to spend some time talking about how to get people motivated to donate to our two charities. It always amazes me how clearly I think when I'm running. I think when we're moving, we think better and see things more clearly—maybe it's one of those things that's hard-wired into us.

On the road that first day, we got a small sample of what we would experience over the coming weeks. People came out with copies of *Running Hot* for me to sign, they made donations and were incredibly encouraging. That Southland hospitality that you hear so much about was certainly obvious. One local chap even gave us a delicious lamb roast for our dinner!

Nine hours after starting the day in Bluff, we made our destination of Edendale. The local kindergarten kids had made a huge sign wishing me well on the run, and a chap called Andrew was there waiting for us with freshly made coffee. With day one over, my body was sore and I was looking forward to getting some sleep.

The next morning, as happened every morning on the run, the alarm went off way too early. Andrew, who had brought us the coffee the previous evening, was there to greet us when we got back out on the road just before 6 a.m. This time, he had a big pot of hot porridge ready to warm us up. The hot porridge and warm company made our stop in Edendale really memorable. Another local, Jan, was also there to see us off and she told me that she had read my book and could relate to my story. She also told me that she had lost an incredible 65 kilograms and was now running marathons. It was a story I would hear similar versions of from very different people over the next few weeks, and every time I heard it I found myself being inspired by the people telling the story.

The next few days carried on in much the same way. The mornings were cold, making it extremely tough for me to get going, but as the days warmed up things got a bit easier for me. The generosity of people all along the route continued to amaze me. At one point, somewhere between Edendale and Balclutha, a couple of local farmers, Duncan and Desiree, were out at the gate waiting to meet us. While they were chatting one of our crew members must have asked how far it was to the nearest petrol station. Quick as a flash, Duncan offered to let us fill the tank from his farm supply.

On day 4, we finally hit Dunedin. I'd been really looking forward to it—Dunedin was the site of my first school visit. I spoke to the kids at Opoho Primary School about the K Per Day Challenge and had a run around the playground with them. It was a really welcome break from the grind of being out on the road.

And, boy, what a grind it was that day. The road north out of Dunedin was a 38-kilometre battle through the hills. It took me a lot longer than I expected but I ended the day after 12 hours running and with 73 more kilometres under my belt. The finishing point was in Waikouaiti, where the locals had a whip round at the pub for donations and shouted me a cold beer. That perked me up no end.

Each day when I'd finished running, the crew would put a marker out and take the coordinates of where I'd finished. Then we'd drive to our accommodation for the night. That night we were staying back at the Quest in Dunedin, where they had an ice bath waiting for me. I was almost as pleased to see it as I was to see the beer in Waikouaiti. While jumping into an ice bath is quite an unpleasant experience, it really helped to bring down any inflammation and mend any micro tears that I might have sustained during the day.

Every now and then along the way I'd finish my day's running wherever we were staying. I loved it when that happened as it meant I could have a sleep-in the next morning. Well, not really a sleep-in, but it meant I could get up 5 a.m. instead of 4.30 a.m. Running the kind of distances I was doing, that extra half hour in bed sometimes made all the difference.

The first place it happened was Oamaru. Crawling out the door of the Kingsgate Hotel straight onto the start line was great. I was especially glad of the easy start to the morning because the weather forecast was for lightning and hail that day. I wanted to get north to Timaru as quickly as possible but my legs had other ideas. They were so tired they wouldn't move as quickly as I wanted them to.

The run between Oamaru and Timaru was quite action-packed. Well, as action-packed as it gets when I'm running at a pace of about 9 kilometres an hour. Getting out in the countryside on a run like this exposes you to the best and worst of people. At one point during the day, we came across a calf that was all tangled up in a rope and making a hell of a noise. Jason and Mitch jumped out of the crew car and freed it, which cheered me up. I needed cheering as I had been quite traumatised a bit earlier when I scared a mother duck waddling along the side of the road with her ducklings. She took off onto the road and was run over by a car. Small things like that are really upsetting when you're at the edge of your physical and mental endurance—a state that wasn't helped when some absolute loser driving past threw a full bottle of Powerade at me. It's hard to understand the mentality of people like that, but luckily I didn't come across too many of them as I made my way north. For every dickhead like that, there were heaps of people who were really positive about what I was trying to do.

After a night in Timaru and a book signing at Paper Plus, I was happy to mark the end of my first week on the road. I was not so happy to still be on the road after 11 hours and only have completed 61 kilometres. It was around this point that I really started to battle with shin splints—an affliction that stayed with me for the rest of the run. Also things were made a bit tougher that day as Mitch left to head back to New Plymouth. I'd loved sharing some of this adventure with my brother, although I'm pretty sure he'll be happy if he never has to come out on the road with me again. After saying goodbye to Mitch, the crew dropped down to two when Jason came down with the flu. Doing a run like this, I couldn't risk catching anything so he was quarantined to the campervan for the day.

Running into Ashburton has to have been one of the highlights of the whole trip. Jarrod Ross from the Tinwald Rugby Club organised a bunch of young club members to run the 18 kilometres between Hinds and Ashburton with me. One of the guys, Dean Watson, was a typical burly young Kiwi bloke who had never run any kind of distance in his life but, alongside me that day, he ran his first half marathon without even realising it. Impressive!

The warm welcome in Ashburton helped me to forget about my shin splints and the problems I'd been having with my hamstrings. I was also stoked to hit the 550-kilometre mark. I'm all about celebrating the milestones while out on the road and 550 felt like a big enough one—it meant I was quarter of the way through the campaign.

With Christchurch in my sights, Jaron headed home and Eileen and Megan joined the team. Megan brought a couple of walking poles with her and they made a hell of a difference. They helped keep me balanced and upright while easing some of the pressure off my legs. Doing long distances was really starting to take its toll on me physically.

Running through Christchurch, like all the cities along the route, was quite tricky. It's always hard to negotiate main highways and condensed traffic when you're used to being out on the open road. The cityscape tends to slow me down slightly, too, so I was happy when we'd cleared the city limits.

It was just north of the city, approaching the township of Amberley, that one of the more hilarious episodes of the whole run occurred. I suddenly found myself really desperate to go to the toilet. On a run like this, there's no airs and graces. When you've got to go, you've got to go. I made a quick dash behind a bush and was just going about my business when I thought I saw something out the corner of my eye. As you can imagine, my legs were pretty shaky and unstable and as I jumped in fright I lost my footing and did a backwards roly-poly down a bank—with my pants around my ankles. As I crawled back up the bank, pulling my pants up, I couldn't help but wonder how the hell I get myself into these situations!

That little tumble sure didn't help my physical state but Megan managed to find someone to help me out. As we were passing through Amberley, she saw a sign for the local physiotherapist. She gave them a call and before long the lovely Bridget Ford was out on the road with me. She gave me a great roadside physio session and strapped my hamstrings and back with kinesio tape to help me make it through the day. I remember wishing we could have taken her with us the rest of the way in the campervan!

By this point, it was getting harder and harder to get out on the road each morning. I found myself in a weird predicament where my right leg seemed to want to walk and my left leg wanted to run. As a result I devised a weird-looking personalised designer shuffle. Even though I was constantly battling myself to keep running and work through the pain, the one thing that kept me going was thinking of all the kids that would be helped by the money I was raising.

Out on the road, Megan's support sometimes extended beyond what would normally be expected. When we were going over the Hundalee Hills, about 40 kilometres south of Kaikoura, my shin splints were so bad I could barely flex my feet. As a result, I found climbing the monster hills nowhere near as painful as going back down them. I tried going down forwards—no good. I tried going down sideways—nope, still painful. Then Megan suggested that I go down backwards. I wasn't quite sure how that was going to work until Megan got in front of me, put her arm around my waist and guided me down the hill. We must have looked like the pushmi-pullyu from Doctor Doolittle! As I was running backwards down the hill, the pain in my legs was so bad I was crying. But when I got to the bottom I couldn't stop laughing. The looks on the faces of some of the truckies who passed us were absolutely priceless.

It was at around this point that Megan started talking seriously to me about cutting back the number of kilometres I was doing each day. From her medical training, she could see that if I tried to carry on at the pace I was going, I was never going to make it to the other end of the country. It was hard for me to hear, but in the end I had to agree with her. We rejigged the schedule. Now, instead of doing the run in 33 days I was going to take 43 days. I was gutted that my body was breaking, but my spirit was still so strong that I knew rescheduling was the only answer.

It was at around this point we passed the 700-kilometre mark. Eleven days down and now 32 to go. We had a quiet celebration over lunch. One of the questions I found a lot of people asked me during the NZ Run was about what kind of food I ate each day.

I get kind of bored eating the same things all the time so I tried to vary my food intake as much as I could. In the morning, I always wanted things that weren't too heavy on my stomach. I tended to crave sweet things early in the day so pikelets, raspberry buns and donated home-baking were big favourites on the menu in the early hours.

We all stopped for lunch each day and I tended to have

filled rolls with plenty of meat to keep my protein intake up followed by whatever fruit we had on hand. Later in the afternoon, the salt cravings would kick in so I'd nibble crisps, pretzels or nuts as I was running. My favourite meal of the day was always dinner. It meant that my day of running was over and I could refuel my body. Eileen's fettuccine became a real dinnertime favourite for me out on the road. Apologies, Eileen, but it's hard to go past the big crayfish we were given by the team at Take Note in Kaikoura as the best meal of the trip.

Running through Kaikoura we struck our first really cold, rainy weather. While I hated running in it, I found that my body felt better than I expected. I think maybe the cold acted like a giant ice pack on my whole body!

Kaikoura was another town that really got behind the project. While I was there a bunch of students from Kaikoura High School came out and ran with me. Then I headed out to Hapuka Primary School, where one of the teacher aides, Carolyn Vasta, had organised for me to go and talk to the kids. As I got closer to the school I could hear a chant of 'Go Lisa, go! Go Lisa, go!' drifting up to greet me.

I really enjoyed sitting down with the children and talking with them about what I was doing and answering all their questions. But always, for me, the best thing was the run around the school sports field with the children joining me. At Hapuka Primary School, like all the rest, they certainly were a boisterous group, full of energy and excitement. One special student at Hapuka School was a boy called Taj who had already had his own cancer battles to deal with in his short life. It was really special meeting him.

With the decrease in kilometres and the increase in time I had to rest, by the time I was running north out of Kaikoura, my running style was nearly back to normal. After the nutty shuffle of a few days earlier, this came as a huge relief. Another massive boost for me was the moment on day 14 when I finally saw the North Island come into view. Crossing Cook Strait was always going to be a huge morale boost for me so knowing it was so close gave me a real buzz.

At one point during the day, Megan and I were running along and a massive gust of wind caught us. It was so strong that it almost knocked me over. Thank goodness Megan was there and, once again, her lightning fast jujitsu-trained reactions stopped me from getting injured. Thankfully, this time she wasn't rescuing me from a venomous snake! Even though Megan caught me I still managed to graze my knee and tweak my left shin. On top of the ever present shin-splint pain, it was horrible.

When we got to Blenheim, Nadene joined the team. She thought she was coming with us for two weeks but somehow it turned into three! Also, while we were staying in Blenheim I got the surprise of my life when my old mate Macca turned up out of the blue. He had planned to run the North Island with me but was still under doctor's orders not to run and his leg was still in a moon boot. Macca, being Macca, reckoned he'd still run some of the way just as long as I didn't tell his doctor! I reckon Jason was about as happy to see Macca as I was—he finally had another bloke on the team to back him up against the four of us girls.

The road between Blenheim and Picton was super hilly but the beautiful scenery and the proximity to the North Island almost made up for that. My shins and hamstrings had started to come right but then my back started spasming. There's always bloody something . . .

My last day of running in the South Island was a short

36 kilometres to the ferry terminal in Picton. With about 15 kilometres to go, we were joined by ultrarunner Richard Law, his daughter Mia and their dog, Buzz. Mia had a friend who was battling cancer so they decided to run with me to show their support.

When we got to Picton Ferry Terminal, Mum had organised a red tinsel finish line. Running through it with Richard, Mia and my crew was a fantastic feeling—950 kilometres . . . done. Tomorrow . . . the North Island and the longest home stretch ever.

In Picton we met up with Hannah, Lana and Anna from CanTeen, who joined us for the ferry trip across to Wellington. As we were checking in at the Interislander counter, the lady organising our tickets said, 'Oh, you're the ones doing the fun run!' I almost cracked up. This run was a lot of things but fun wouldn't be the first word I'd use to describe it.

After being invited up onto the bridge to meet the captain, the crew found me a bed in the ferry's sick bay so I could rest up for the duration of the trip. It was a great opportunity to chat with the girls from CanTeen. Hearing their stories and knowing what they had been through gave me a bit of a wake-up call. I realised that if the worst thing facing me that day was a 30-kilometre run north out of Wellington then I was pretty bloody lucky.

Our welcome in Wellington was pretty amazing, with TV cameras and the deputy mayor there to greet us. David and Ang from our sponsors Big Media also joined the crew in Wellington, so there was quite a bunch of us as we headed north.

Our first full day running in the North Island started at 5.25 a.m. when Macca, Nadene and me piled into the crew car and headed up the road to our starting point on the Kapiti Coast. The road north out of Wellington is really narrow so I ran a lot of it by myself, which gave me some time to reflect on the previous seventeen days' running and take in the beautiful scenery.

Those few moments of peace didn't last long though. The air was filled with what sounded like about 4000 motorbikes. The only thing louder than 4000 motorbikes is 4000 motorbikes tooting their horns! A huge group of bikers were out for a morning ride and when they saw me their hands went straight into their wallets and our donation buckets filled up really fast. That sure as hell woke me up.

A bit further along the road, though, I got to see the flipside of human nature once again. The road was so narrow that Macca and Nadene would drive ahead of me and pull into passing bays to wait for me. Never one to sit still, Macca would usually drop to the ground and do press-ups on these stops, which I'm sure passing motorists found amusing. Well, most of them.

One lady had slowed down to watch me running and then slowed again and waved to the crew as she passed. This clearly infuriated the man in the car behind her and he decided to stop and take it out on Macca and Nadene. I saw him pass where they were parked then pull his car over and get out. Oh, crap. He stormed back to where they were and I could see that he was absolutely nutting off at them. Eventually, he went back to his car and drove off. When I caught up with Nadene and Macca, they reckoned he was screaming at them for holding up traffic. Even when Macca explained to him that it was a run for children's charities, he just kept swearing at them. I hope he never needs the help of the charities that I was raising money for.

One of the things I learned to dread on the NZ Run was rain during the night. Getting out running in the morning when the shoulder of the road was underwater was a total nightmare. It meant I had to be twice as careful about where I was going and I had to contend with the exposure to the water softening my feet and causing blisters.

It was in these horrible wet conditions that I ran into Levin. Even though it was pouring with rain, a guy called Adrian Henare came out to run with me. I wasn't feeling the best but we got chatting and Adrian told me that I was a hero to him. It was an incredibly humbling thing for me to hear and his timing could not have been better. Adrian gave me the turboboost I needed to complete a tough day's running in the rain. Throughout the run I was really touched by the number of people who came out and ran with me, sharing some of their own stories along the way.

It was around this point in the run that I met Palmerston North physiotherapist Carol Armitage. She did a fantastic job of restrapping my leg with kinesio tape. Then she did something completely genius. She cut out a pattern for us to use so that whenever I needed retaping one of my crew members would be able to do it for me. Lifesaver.

My days of running settled into something of a pattern through the lower North Island. I got loads of support from locals, the donations rolled in and plenty of keen runners joined me out on the road. It was at about this point that I started to see running as a job. I couldn't imagine not getting up, putting my shoes on and running 50 kilometres every day. It was a pretty cool headspace to be in.

My third week on the road started in Turakina, took me through Whanganui and ended in Maxwell. For the first time, my dad, Cyril, joined the crew on the road. Typically, it wasn't long before he ran into someone he knew. Dad was sitting at the side of the road waiting for me when his old mate Charles

Osbourne, father of ex-All Black Glen Osbourne, drove up. No worries about parking the car for Charles. He just stopped in the middle of the road to have a yarn to his old mate Cyril, much to the surprise and annoyance of the people in the car behind him!

Getting going on day 22 was a real struggle but one thought kept me going—today, I was going to be home in Taranaki. And Taranaki sure turned it on for me.

On the road between Waverley and Patea the then-mayor of Whanganui, Michael Laws, joined me for a few kilometres. His young daughter had cancer and he was impressed with what I was doing. Michael later organised a civic reception for me in Whanganui, where I was presented with a beautiful glass waka (a Maori canoe).

Heading into the outskirts of Patea, I was feeling really low. But when I got into town, the place was buzzing. There were people everywhere and they'd all come out to support me. There, in Patea, I met one of the most inspiring people of my whole run. Shyly leaning on his car outside his house was a guy called Mike Kanara. He talked to my crew and asked if it would be OK if he came along and ran with us for 1.5 kilometres. Of course, we welcomed him to the team and, as we ran, Mike and I got chatting. He told me that he had lost 13 kilograms in the last seven weeks and that he was determined to turn his life around. He'd joined the gym and was doing weights but he still found running tough. His best distance to date had been 5 kilometres. We kept chatting and Mike kept running. The man who had planned to run 1.5 kilometres with me ended up doing 16 kilometres—his personal best and, boy, was he surprised to learn he could do that distance. When we reached Kakaramea Pub that night, everyone came out to meet us and we all ended up in the pub having a beer. Mike was named 'player of the day'.

The next morning I couldn't help wondering how Mike was feeling but I was buzzing at seeing how stoked he had been with what he'd achieved. Being back in Taranaki meant my brothers, Mitch and Dawson, and Mum and Dad all came out to join the crew. Typically, Mitch and Dawson went straight for the fridge in the campervan and completely ransacked it. Thankfully, Nadene had hidden the homemade banana cake I'd been given the night before in the microwave—she guessed correctly they'd never think to look in there!

Just as my day's running was about to finish, the clouds parted and I saw a sight I'd been longing for: Mount Taranaki, and it was perfect as ever. I always feel as if I draw power from the mountain and seeing it that day gave me the strength to continue my quest.

Just as seeing the mountain gave me a much-needed boost, I was running into New Plymouth and it was awesome. In New Plymouth I was greeted by the mayor, Peter Tennent, before heading to Puke Ariki and meeting up with students from Sacred Heart, Manukorihi Intermediate, Waitara High School and New Plymouth Girls High School. After talking to a great group of Taranaki young people, I headed over to a local rest home where they had taken on my K Per Day Challenge.

I also met up with Kelvin and Craig from The Frontrunner store in town. They were impressed to hear that I'd gone through four pairs of running shoes in 24 days. They reckoned it was probably a record for shoes from their store!

I spent a night at home in my own bed and allowed myself a late start the next day. A group from Waitara High School gave me a rousing haka to send me on my way. It was brilliant to have such strong support as today would be the day I had to tackle Mount Messenger.

At Motunui, the whole school was out waiting for me and when I stopped to greet the kids, they all did a haka for me. It was a cool way to be farewelled on the road out of Taranaki.

When I got there, I saw that some guys from a Works Infrastructure roading gang had put out traffic warning signs for me. The run over Mount Messenger was made so much easier by those guys and I felt really well looked after.

Dad was back on the crew for the run through to Awakino. It was great having him with me through Mokau, which is a really special place for him, but I was a bit suspicious to see his fishing rod in the back of his ute though. The kids at Mokau School had been doing the K Per Day Challenge and joined me for a run through town. Jason was really worried because some of them didn't have shoes on. I assured him they were 'Naki kids and they were tough!

The Awakino Gorge was always going to be a difficult piece of road for us to negotiate. It's really narrow in parts and, being the main road north out of New Plymouth, there's often a lot of traffic on it. Megan and I hit the road early to get through the gorge before the traffic built up too much. But when I arrived at the Awakino tunnel, which was always going to be a bit scary to run through, I'd lost Megan and the Prius. It turned out she'd had to stop for a pee and that left me taking on the tunnel alone. Thankfully, a truckie in a milk tanker realised what was going on and drove slowly behind me stopping all the traffic so I could run through the tunnel safely. New Zealand truckies might get a bit of a hard time, but there are some cool dudes out there and I hugely appreciated their support and courtesy to me at all times while I was on the road.

Once we got through the tunnel, the rest of the crew caught up with us. As I was running, I came across a hawk on the road that had a broken wing. I stopped and waited for Megan and Jaron, asking them for help to rescue the hawk. Megan grabbed a towel and tried to pick the bird up. It was less than happy at the prospect, but eventually Megan gathered it up and put it in the car. The only problem then was what to do with it. Fortunately, Vicky Kjestrup from Mahanui offered to take it to the Otorohanga Kiwi House where they'd be able to look after it.

After the excitement of the hawk rescue, the rest of the day was pretty quiet, in real contrast to my days of running through Taranaki. My body was still feeling quite good but my hips were starting to niggle a wee bit. Still, not bad considering I'd run more than 1400 kilometres and was held together by tape and glue.

Four weeks on the road had now ticked over and on day 28, my main mission was to find out how my mate, the hawk, had fared. Out on the road, however, it felt like half of Taranaki were on a pilgrimage to Auckland to see Pearl Jam play, but it was great to get all their toots of support and their donations.

I got a couple of important phone calls on day 28. The first was to tell me that Howard Dell, who had checked himself out of hospital to crew for me at Death Valley, had finally undergone his liver transplant surgery. I thought a lot about Howard that day, praying that he'd be OK.

The second call was from my ex-husband, Gerhard. He had undertaken a similar run in Austria and said he'd heard a rumour that I had shortened the route I was planning to run. Cheeky bugger! I told him in no uncertain terms that it might be taking me longer but that I'd be running the full 2200 kilometres.

When I got to Otorohanga I found out that the hawk had been too badly damaged to save and had been euthanised. I was a bit sad about it but figured that at least we'd given it the best chance we could.

Leaving Otorohanga the next morning, Megan and I started to worry that we had a stalker. We first noticed him parked outside as we loaded the crew vehicle. Then when we left to drive to the start line for the day, he followed us in his car. We were a bit nervous so pulled into a car park by a café and he carried on past. False alarm, or so we thought . . . until we drove around the corner and there he was waiting for us again. We carried on driving and managed to lose him. Whew! Until Dad came out to meet us on the road. We told him about our weird experience and he started to laugh. Apparently the guy had driven back to the motel and talked to Dad—he just wanted his book signed! He was just too shy to ask.

After a bit of a strange start, good news came that day in the form of word that Howard was recovering well from his surgery—so much so that he was sending his own emails. Another bit of good news was that Jaron and his Taranaki Surf League Team had won the Taranaki Sports Team of the Year award the previous night in New Plymouth. I tell you, I was surrounded by absolute champions.

My brother Dawson brought Mum back up to meet us on the road between Otorohanga and Pirongia. Mum was back with the crew after two days at home. Dawson spent a few hours with us before he headed off to Auckland. For us, Auckland was still three days away.

As I ran into Huntly I was met by my friend Jackie and her daughter Chloe. Jackie ran with me for an hour as we ran through Huntly then the two of them joined the crew for our evening meal. That night we stayed at an outdoor retreat where we could relax around the barbecue and catch up.

With my body finally adjusted to being on the road every day, the kilometres really started to feel like they were falling away. There's that old joke about Aucklanders not knowing life exists south of the Bombay Hills. Having run over them, I can see why. Those things are BIG and they really took a lot out of my legs. Before I knew it I was on the outskirts of Auckland, which meant only one thing—traffic, and lots of it.

In the rest of the country, starting early meant avoiding the traffic. Not in Auckland though. The morning commuter rush goes from about 6 a.m. until about 9 every day. It was tough to run in and I stuck to the footpaths where I could. I had one near miss when I checked carefully before setting out to cross a busy road. Suddenly a car came flying across three lanes of traffic and nearly knocked me over. It made me wary for the rest of the day.

Jaron and Megan both left me in Auckland and headed back to New Plymouth. Megan had been staring at maps for days on end plotting my course for the coming days so was probably happy to get back to work.

On my second day of running in Auckland, I got up really early, but not to go running. It felt really weird. Instead, I was being interviewed on TVNZ's *Breakfast* show. I was a bit nervous about being interviewed by Paul Henry, but being told I had great legs on national television sure helped to calm the nerves.

By the time I got on the road, it was already 10 a.m. It was a typical Auckland day—humid, hot and raining. And there were hills, boy, were there hills. There were so many of them it did my head in. It was a really tough day for me as it was the day that, had we stuck to our original schedule, we would have been finishing the run. I had to apologise to the crew at the end of the day for being grumpy, but some days the psychological struggle was bigger for me than the physical one, and that was just one of those days.

Over the next couple of days my mood improved but the terrain didn't. From Auckland pretty much all the way to Whangarei it was up and down hills the whole way.

With 320 kilometres to go to the finish, I had a night away from the road to fulfil a promise to my mates at the Tinwald Rugby Club in Ashburton. I flew to Christchurch to take part in a fundraiser for Jarrod and the boys that I'd committed to before we changed my running schedule. Alongside me on the stage were boxer Shane Cameron, former All Black Frank Bunce, and Welsh storyteller Phil Kingsley Jones. It was a great night, but it felt kind of weird being in the South Island again.

The following day I flew back north to Kaitaia, where Mum and Nadene met me at the airport and we headed up to Cape Reinga—the northernmost tip of the North Island. It might seem like a bit of a weird diversion, but we wanted to finish the run in Auckland and, to make the logistics of that work, I would run the section from the far north of the island back to just south of Whangarei so as to run into Auckland for the scheduled finish. With so much going on, I barely had time to register that I only had one more week left out on the road.

Restarting my run at Cape Reinga lighthouse and heading south gave me absolutely spectacular views, and it was well worth the extra kilometre it took. At that point Mum, Jason and Nadene were on the crew and I think they got a bit overexcited about the lighthouse and forgot about me. I was running along on my own when I really needed to stop for a toilet break. No crew means no toilet paper. There was only one thing for it—use whatever is to hand. It was then that I found out that the native toitoi grass in Northland is way softer than the variety that grows in Taranaki!

While in the far north we stayed at the Puki Nui Motel and campsite, where we met Pete and Shelley. I'd gone to school with Shelley in Bell Block when we were kids and it was great to see her again. She'd been working her magic on the whole community up there and managed to raise $2000 for my charities. But that wasn't all: Shelley also managed to run 30 kilometres with me.

The Puki Nui Fishing Club invited our crew for dinner and we spent a fantastic night there, eating fresh fish while looking out over the Houhora Harbour.

As I ran through Northland, I started to notice that everything up there seemed to be oversized. We saw some absolutely huge bulls, some massive free-range turkeys, and really big old trees. This weird gigantism was even evident in the food when I saw the biggest donuts and apple slices I'd ever come across in a bakery in Kaitaia. Unfortunately, the same could be said for the hills up there. Some of them were really nasty. At least the views from the top made it worth the struggle.

Thankfully there was very little traffic on the roads around the north, which made running way easier for me. It was so quiet up there that we could always hear any cars coming our way and get off the road. Jason, as an American, found running down the middle of the road rather stressful.

Some other people that might have been a bit stressed-out by our presence in the area were the residents of one of the local gang pads. One morning Mum realised that she had forgotten to clear the odometer in the car that morning to track the distance I was running. It meant she had to backtrack to where I'd started. In order to turn the car around she pulled into the nearest driveway, which happened to be a gang headquarters. And she had a flashing traffic warning light on the roof of the car! It was just before seven in the morning and I can only imagine what went on inside the house before some-one looked out to see that what looked like a police raid was just my mum driving a Toyota Prius slowly and sporting a red bandana.

On the road into Kaeo, I struggled a bit with a stomach upset and my hips were really starting to play up, too. I think the continuous pounding on the road was finally starting to take its toll on me. Knowing that I only had four more days on the road was only just enough to keep me positive and keep me moving. There was no way I could give up so close to the end.

Even though my hips were really sore, on day 40 I finally managed to get rid of the kinesio tape that had been holding my back and legs together since I'd first been strapped way back in Amberley. I was blown away at how my body had coped with the punishment I had given it and how it had still managed to repair itself. I could barely believe that a month ago I had had to walk down that hill in the Hundalees back-wards supported by Megan.

When we were overnighting in Kerikeri, we got one of our biggest treats of the whole trip. Colin Ashton from the award-winning restaurant Food at Wharepuke invited us all to dine at his restaurant. The mix of European and Thai cuisine all served in a sub-tropical garden was absolutely heavenly and a much appreciated break from the grind of being on the road.

It wasn't long, though, before we again went from the sublime to the ridiculous. The following day, I was running wearing a buff covering my face—something I often do when my lungs are a bit sore or I feel like I am going to get a bit wheezy. The NZ Run buffs were bright red. Nadene had a matching one in her hair, and Mum had hers around her arm to stop it from getting sunburnt while she was driving.

What hadn't even occurred to us was that in some parts of the country, it's not really done to wear the Mongrel Mob colour of red in an area dominated by the Black Power gang, whose colour is blue. Anyway, after so many days on the road, none of us ever worried when a car slowed down next to us. People quite often stopped to give us donations or to ask us what we were doing. This particular day, a white car stopped and Nadene started running over to the car to answer questions and take donations. Then I watched her come to a screaming halt. The car was full of these really staunch look-ing dudes. And they weren't happy.

But when they looked at us all a bit closer, they just looked a bit confused. They drove off and came back a few times as if they were trying to work out what to do about us. Finally they left us alone. It wasn't really until the end of the day and the three of us had the chance to talk about it that we realised how much trouble we could have been in.

Given the hilly terrain in Northland, I started to look forward to being back in Auckland's traffic. I felt like I was permanently climbing or descending hills the whole time I was out on the road. But even the hills, my hips and the heat couldn't dampen the rising excitement among the team. The countdown was definitely on . . .

With a couple of days to go, the crew started to loosen up a bit and their lack of sleep became apparent. It didn't take much before we were all laughing hysterically for no rea-son. I was really glad that we were all still having a good time together after such a long time spent living in each other's pockets.

After finishing the day's running in Waro, just north of Whangarei, Nadene, Mum and I headed into town on a mis-sion of a completely different kind. I was determined to get a new outfit to wear at my homecoming in New Plymouth on Sunday. I quickly found the perfect dress at the perfect price and it was nice to be thinking about something other than running for a little while.

Once we'd completed our shopping mission, Nadene said she'd go back and get the car then come and pick us up. Mum and I waited and waited—no Nadene. She finally arrived back about 15 minutes later with a pretty good reason for having stood us up. She got back to the car just to see it being winched onto a tow truck. No matter what she said to the driver— and she's a good fast talker—there was no way she could get out of paying the $165 fine and towing fees. Stink one . . . but at least I had a new dress.

With only two more days on the road to go, I started to think about what it would be like to stop and rest. Most of my body had sorted itself out but my hips were still causing me agony. They were at their worst when I started running again after a food or toilet break so I tried to keep these to a minimum.

South of Whangarei, there was a long section of road works. There was a road gang there and cars were having to wait in long queues. Nadene saw her chance and got among the stationary vehicles rattling the donation bucket. She's nothing if not cheeky, that girl. While Nadene racked up the total, I just kept on running. There wasn't a Stop–Go man in the country who could have stopped me so close to realising my dream.

Blissfully, there were several long flat straights on the road that day and I'd almost forgotten what it felt like to run on the flat. With the traffic slowed to a crawl, quite a few people would ask me where I was running to. They didn't seem that impressed when I told them I was just going south a bit, but their faces when I told them I'd run from Bluff were pretty funny. It was surreal to me that in a few short kilometres I'd finally be finished what had seemed almost impossible all those days ago just outside Amberley when Megan had to rejig the schedule.

When I finally reached the spot that I'd finished at before I flew to Ashburton, I gladly jumped into the crew van and we headed south to Torbay on Auckland's North Shore. With one more day to go, I wasn't sure I'd be able to sleep—I was so excited.

But sleep I did and day 43 dawned a bit drizzly and overcast. Getting on the road, I ran along the coast through Auckland's East Coast Bays. Sadly we weren't able to run across the Harbour Bridge but I got to do the next best thing. At Devonport on the North Shore, we were all joined by Faye Smythe and Ben Mitchel (aka 'TK' Tuhaka Samuels) from the TV show *Shortland Street*. Another Kiwi champion came to our rescue—Olympic kayaking gold medallist Ian Ferguson, who owns Ferg's Kayaks, supplied kayaks and all the gear for us to paddle from Devonport over to his kayaking school in Mission Bay.

For a while it looked like the harbour crossing might get cancelled because of the weather but I reckon if it had I would have tried to swim across—I was so determined to make that finish line that day.

Paddling from Devonport was a beautiful way to get from one side of the city to the other. When we got to Mission Bay there was a group of about fifty runners all waiting to escort me the last 5 kilometres to the Hilton on Auckland's waterfront. What a buzz! I'd come 2245 kilometres and for the last five, I was in the middle of a pack of super-supportive runners. Amazing feelings all round.

As I crossed the finish line, there was Murray Dick who'd

started the run with me in Bluff 43 days before. This time he was leading a rousing haka. Nothing I've done before or since could match the elation I felt at being welcomed like that.

The Hilton put on an amazing welcoming party for me where a crowd of my sponsors, supporters, family and friends were waiting. And even though I was absolutely knackered, there was no way this girl was having an early night. For the first time in forty-three days, I put on a pair of high heels and danced the night away! I'd done it. The one big goal I'd had all my life was complete and, boy, did I celebrate!

But it wasn't over yet . . . The next morning, I flew back down to New Plymouth with Jason, Murray Dick and his wife, Jane. On the plane, we decided we'd all run the final leg together—it seemed quite fitting considering we'd all been there at the start line together, too.

Landing at New Plymouth airport, I was blown away by the huge crowd of supporters who were waiting there to greet me. Many of them joined Murray, Jason and me for the final 7-kilometre run from the airport to the Puke Ariki Landing in town. It was great to see Megan again—and to see that she couldn't let her organiser's role go as she provided the group of runners with a final safety briefing before we all hit the road into the city. All along the road supporters were tooting, waving and cheering me on. There is nowhere else quite like Taranaki for me and all these people made sure that I knew that I was home.

The closer we got to Puke Ariki Landing, the more runners joined the pack. Finally, I could see Mayor Pete standing there waiting for me. We all ran, laughing, cheering, arms in the air. I was home. This was the end of the road.

I had done it—I'd crossed the finish line. All those days and nights, all the work, the pain, the organising and arranging, and there I was having conquered the beast. How did I feel? I'm not sure I have the words to describe it even now. I was numb, excited, exhausted, but most of all, so very grateful. Grateful to my amazing crew, grateful to all the people who helped and supported me along the way, grateful to everyone who donated money to my charities, grateful to my family for always backing me in my mad schemes, and grateful to have finished.

Crewing advice from Megan and Nadene

When you're racing, if you've got a crew or people that you're running with, the bonds that you develop are on a different level than what you normally have—they're very intense. Everyone is struggling together to reach a common goal. Your crew will be running around after you trying to get you to the finish line.

Crewing for an ultrarunner is a really good way to get an insight into the sport, especially if you're considering taking up ultrarunning. Here's some advice for potential crew members from two of my awesome crewies—Megan Stewart and Nadene George. Megan crewed at Death Valley in 2009 and on the NZ Run. Since then she has run the Atacama and Sahara desert races herself. She describes her experience in the 4 Deserts Sahara Race on page 128. Nadene crewed on the NZ Run and still runs with me as often as she can.

Megan's story

Be prepared for anything. Be prepared for everything. Do your homework. Ultimately, it's a team thing and you need to have a team that works well, trains well and plays well together. Everybody needs to know their role and every person on the team needs to have something unique that they offer the crew.

You need to have one person on the team that keeps their eye on the bigger picture and has got their finger on the pulse of everybody else's roles and responsibilities. Otherwise everyone gets so involved in what's going on nobody sees the bigger picture. If you're in the middle of something you can't see everything, but if you stay a little bit outside of what's going on you get a much clearer picture of everything that's going on and what needs to be done.

Nadene's story

It's not just the athlete that has to pick themselves up and start every day. You'll have tough days too and you have to look after yourself in order to look after your runner.

To be a good crew member, you have to be really unselfish. The whole focus has to be on the runner and what they need. It's not about you at all. If you're the sort of person who likes a lot of attention, forget about it. It's your job to make sure the runner does exactly what they're meant to be doing. You always have to protect them from anything that's going to stop them from completing their race. Sometimes that involves protecting them from spectators and supporters. Sometimes it can be protecting them from other crew members. And sometimes it can be protecting them from themselves.

You need to know your athlete well enough to be able to tell what they need and when, because sometimes they won't know that themselves.

You have to be pretty fit but you will probably surprise yourself with what you're capable of. Because you're not focusing on yourself and your own running, you'll end up achieving much more and running further than you ever thought possible.

Crewing is hard work and you've got to realise that things don't always go to plan. You've got to be able to react to changes really quickly.

People sometimes ask me what I get out of crewing for Lisa. I love being part of a team that helps her to achieve incredible things. I've also learned a hell of a lot from her when it comes to my own running. I realised pretty quickly that I should watch what she was doing and copy her. If she had an ice bath at the end of the day, then I did, too. It really helped me to stay in good condition while I was supporting her. I'd also keep a close eye on what Lisa was eating and drinking while she was running. I never used to eat or drink while I was running but I do now because that's what Lisa does. It's made a huge difference to my stamina while I'm out there.

Crewing for Lisa made me realise that I was capable of doing a lot more than I thought I was. It was amazing to be involved in it for the charity—getting money off people for a good cause made it really fun. Whenever I'm low and I'm pushing my limits, I think about Lisa. What she has achieved is a real inspiration for me to push myself a bit harder.

4

Into the Gobi Desert

The human spirit needs physical movement more than the body does. Watch someone on the telephone—they'll pace or move about in their chair if they are sitting down. We think better, we talk better, we express ourselves better when we're moving.

The Gobi March, 27/6 – 3/7/2010

It took a long time for my body to recover from the constant stress of running for forty-three days in a row after the NZ Run campaign. As is usual after a big project, it also took me a while to get my head around the fact that this huge goal I'd been working towards for so long was now achieved.

Once the euphoria of completing a big challenge like this dies down, I often find that I get a bit down and struggle to adjust back to everyday life. I've found that the best cure for the post-event blues is to start planning the next challenge.

Given the physical toll that running the length of the country had taken on me, I knew I couldn't take on anything too big for at least six months. I also knew that I needed something that would really challenge me. I gave it a lot of thought and did a bit of research into races that would be happening in mid-2010. After completing the second Death Valley campaign and the NZ Run, I decided it was a good time to go back to multi-day stage races. Partly, this was because I couldn't afford the expense of taking a full crew with me again. As usual, I was drawn back to my first love—desert running.

There's something about being out in a stark, arid landscape so far from urban life that I just can't get enough of. I love the different challenges that desert running brings. Out there, it's just me and the landscape.

The obvious place for me to head was the Sahara, as that's where I've done the bulk of my desert running over the years. But having already done the Marathon des Sables in Morocco, the Trans 333 in Niger and an unassisted crossing of the Libyan Desert in Egypt, I decided that it was time to strike out somewhere new. That was when I heard about the Gobi March.

Organised by a company called Racing the Planet, the Gobi March is held annually in June in the Gobi Desert in China. It's a seven-day, six-stage, 250-kilometre race that consists of four one-day stages, one long stage that can take runners up to two days—known as the Long March—and the final day which is just 10 kilometres.

The race takes place in the Gobi Desert in north-western China near the border with Mongolia and Kazakhstan. The Gobi is the largest desert in Asia and the world's fifth largest. I was less than thrilled to find out that it's also the windiest place in the world outside of the north and south poles. Even though it's officially a desert, the landscape there varies from sandy desert to wide open plains and mountains. With variety like that, I knew this race would provide me with the challenge I was looking for.

The Gobi March was first run in 2003 and was founded in honour of three English Christian missionaries who lived and worked in China early last century. Until 1923, these three women, Mildred Cable and the sisters Eva and Francesca French, initially worked in the more accessible Shanxi province. Then, when they were all in their fifties, they decided to strike out into a more remote part of China. Much to the concern of their colleagues, the trio made their way to the largely Muslim part of north-western China. It took several months for them to reach the Gobi Desert, where they based themselves for the next thirteen years.

Once there, they travelled all over the Gobi region, with the mission of not only converting the local people to Christianity but also looking after orphaned children, providing basic medical care and trying to ensure that local girls received an education. Life for the three women was never easy but they rose to every challenge they met along the way. Mildred Cable described the Gobi:

> Only a fool crosses the great Gobi without misgivings. In this trackless waste, where every restriction is removed and where you are beckoned and lured in all directions . . . One narrow way is the only road for you. In the great and terrible wilderness, push on with eyes blinded to the deluding mirage, your ears deaf to the call of the seducer, and your mind un-diverted from the goal.

What female ultrarunner could resist entering a race dedicated to three remarkable women who, unwittingly, managed to completely define what it is that we do? Inspired by Mildred

Cable and the French sisters, I knew that the Gobi March had to be my next race. After all, if three fifty-something female missionaries could cross the Gobi without any of the modern luxuries we'd have on the race, then surely I could do it, too.

Once I'd decided that the Gobi was for me, I spent the next few months pulling together sponsorship and sorting out all the visas and gear I'd need for the race. I also talked with Peter Tainui at Maori Television and we decided that I'd make a documentary about the race while I was out there. Before I knew it, I was in Hong Kong.

Like most Kiwis around the world on 21 June 2010, I found the nearest bar that was showing live FIFA World Cup coverage. I felt right at home in the ex-pat pub full of Kiwis as we cheered the All Whites on to their legendary 1–1 draw against the defenders, Italy. After the game, I felt buoyed by another bunch of Kiwis beating the odds on the international stage. Bring on the Gobi Desert, I say!

From Hong Kong I flew to Shanghai, where I spent a couple of days. While I was there, I was looked after superbly by a fellow Gobi March entrant, John McKenna. John is a Kiwi who has lived in China since 1995. Lucky for me, he has his own travel business—www.Travel-the-Real-China.com. He specialises in showing travellers a side of life in China they wouldn't normally see. John showed me around Shanghai and also helped me out with finding some last-minute supplies I needed for the race.

While I was in Shanghai, I was also invited to speak at an event hosted by New Zealand Trade and Enterprise (NZTE), a government organisation whose role is helping New Zealand businesses grow internationally. It was a real honour to be invited to speak at New Zealand Central, the NZTE hub in Shanghai. I was amazed at just how much being there felt like being at home. My talk was part of a series organised by David Caselli, head of Shanghai-based company NZ China Direct. David is an ultrarunner and he was also part of the strong Kiwi contingent heading to Urumqi for the Gobi March.

Like most people, I don't really love public speaking, but when David told me that other people he'd had speak in this series of 'Great New Zealanders' included Jonah Lomu, Kiri Te Kanawa, Peter Jackson and John Walker, I made sure that I gave it my absolute all—with company like that I certainly didn't want to be the one to let the side down!

The good thing about having to focus on public speaking was that it took my mind off the upcoming race for a little while, but only for a little while. While I was in Shanghai, I found out that the Gobi March included a couple of river crossings. And that can only mean two things—wet feet and blisters.

Before leaving Shanghai, I did a practice run at packing everything I'd need into the North Face backpack I was using for the race. This is never a fun process as it brings home to me just how little I can take out on a race with me. I've got to be able to carry all my food for the seven-day race, which means doing a balancing act to make sure I've got the absolute bare minimum in my pack but still have enough to keep my body functioning while I'm out in the 46°+ heat. Every extra gram in the pack is a burden when I'm running.

From Shanghai, I took a five-hour flight to Urumqi, a city of two million people that has the reputation of being the most remote city in China. Arriving in Urumqi, I felt quite over-whelmed. The combination of jet lag, not having trained for a while, different food and the massive amount of smog in the city meant that I felt quite out of sorts. Often when I'm travel-ling, I am reminded of just how good life is in New Zealand.

Spending time in places like Urumqi always makes me realise how lucky we are at home—being able to see the stars at night and the sun during the day, having fresh water to swim in, clean beaches and soaring mountains as part of our daily life is such a blessing. The more I travel and experience other cultures and ways of life, the more I appreciate home.

Not long after arriving in Urumqi, I met up with a number of other athletes who were also doing the Gobi March. We were a really mixed bunch, ranging from walkers to world-class ultrarunners. It was good to spend time with my fellow competitors and know that we were all there to experience the desert, push our bodies and our abilities, face our many fears, push to the limits and strive for our own goals.

Because of its remoteness and the ethnic mix of Kazakhs, Tajiks, Uygurs and Han Chinese, Urumqi has a bit of a wild west feel to it. While we were there, people were getting ready to mark the first anniversary of the riots that took place in July 2009 in the city. The riots were the culmination of tension between the local Uygur people and the Han Chinese who make up about 90 per cent of China's population. Over several days, clashes between the two groups saw at least 190 people killed and many vehicles and buildings destroyed. It's hard to know what really happened over that time as the Chinese government cut off communications with the outside world until calm had been restored.

What I do know, though, is that the tension in Urumqi was still evident almost a year later. The areas where the riots took place are completely closed to foreigners and the local police kept a close eye on our group of international runners. After the freedom of New Zealand it was a very weird feeling to know I couldn't just go where I wanted, when I wanted.

For the first few days I suffered from quite bad nausea

at night. I'm not sure if that was due to the heavy smog that hung in the air or the radical change in the food I was eating. Either way, the lack of sleep soon started to take its toll on me. Added to that, the heat was really playing havoc with my legs. They swelled up quite badly, unable to cope with the change of temperature from a wintry 5–10° Celsius in Taranaki, to 30° days in Urumqi.

After a few days in Urumqi, I started to go a bit stir crazy. It was good to have time to acclimatise and get over the jet lag but with all the waiting around, I started to get paranoid about every little twinge and ache in my body. I tried to focus on keeping my body as healthy as possible but I couldn't wait to get out into the desert and the forces of nature. All I wanted to do was get started. All of the travel and waiting around were starting to get to me and I knew I just needed to start running.

The lack of opportunities for training while we were in Urumqi were somewhat offset when I found a flash hotel up the road from the more modest one where I was staying. And what do you know? It had a fully equipped gym that I was allowed to use. Getting my body in motion again was the best cure for the nervousness and discomfort I was feeling. Once I started working out, my concerns all started to disappear.

That was until three days before we were due to start racing and the rain started to pour down in Urumqi. Rumours started coming in thick and fast that there were flash floods out in the desert and the route had been washed out. Then talk started about the desert temperatures, with reports of anything from 5° to 55°. None of us were sure what to believe and I couldn't work out whether I'd be dealing with wet shoes and blisters from wading through swollen rivers or sunstroke from the burning hot sun. We'd been told to expect the unexpected and that was all we could do until we got out of the city onto the course.

Two days after the rains came, the athletes all gathered together in Urumqi for the race check-in and registration. We then all piled onto buses and headed north into the Turpan Depression, where the race was due to start the following morning. The Turpan Depression is a deep mountain basin that measures about 28,600 square kilometres. The entire area is below sea level with the lowest point of the basin reaching a massive 154 metres below sea level. The area's history is quite amazing as it was an important point on the ancient Silk Road trading route that was first opened to allow the flow of goods from China into Europe.

En route to our first camp, we were welcomed by the governor and mayor of Turpan before heading on to our first campsite in Gaoyachun village. Nestled amid mountains, it was a very beautiful spot. Given this first stage was called 'Tian Shan mountains' I probably should have guessed what the terrain was going to be like. Just knowing that the first stage was going to be 32 kilometres of mountainous country had me a bit worried and I wasn't sure if my lungs would hold up. I also wondered how I had managed to enter a desert race that landed me in the mountains. I guess when I entered the race I had visions of the vast Mongolian plains, but the Gobi landscape was very different to what I had expected. It was a real mixture of mountains, sand dunes, riverbeds and much more.

Because of the mountain setting, the first night at camp was pretty cold. But the next morning dawned fine and clear, which was a relief after all the worry about rain and flooding that we'd had back in Urumqi. The race started at 7 a.m. and my plan for the day was to not go too hard-out so that I could acclimatise to the conditions. Easing into a race like this is really important—there's no point blowing a gasket on the first day.

The early part of the day was through pasture lands, but then the climbing started. Even though it was only a 32-kilometre stage, that first day was a ridiculous and painful reminder of what it's like to be running in a desert. It almost made me miss those gently rolling hills of Northland that had seemed so challenging in the final stages of the NZ Run. Throughout the first day, I climbed from just below sea level up to 2200 metres over some of the roughest terrain imaginable. I crested mountains only to find that the only way down was to slide down loose shingle. The thought of injury on land like that is never far from my mind.

The sun was really intense and as I climbed higher I started to rely more heavily on my asthma inhaler. The combination of cold and altitude meant that my lungs were working over-time for every scrap of oxygen they could find. The added discomfort of a niggly sciatic nerve made that first day really tough. Reaching the end of the stage at Camp Kazak Pasture, I would have done anything to have a masseur waiting there for me.

Despite my injury niggles it was hard not to notice just how beautiful the country I was running through actually was. Watching wild horses running across the Gobi Desert was one of the most uplifting sights I saw that day. If only I could have been running as effortlessly and freely as they were.

The second day was pretty much a carbon copy of the first—29 kilometres of climb and descent in the mountains. The first 14 kilometres were the worst and they knackered me so much that I didn't really enjoy the rest of the day. I continued to struggle with the altitude out there. Some of the climbs were so steep as to be almost vertical—not easy at the best of times and absolutely brutal with 10 kilograms of gear on your back. Camp Three—called Da He Yan by the locals—was on a clifftop overlooking the appropriately named Never Ending Canyon. That was certainly how it felt at some points out there on the trail that day. I couldn't help thinking that if a 29-kilometre day like that had challenged me so much, what the hell was the long 100-kilometre stage going to be like? It would be fair to say that I was scared. Very scared.

By day three, the worst of the mountain stages were over and leaving Da He Yan Camp we ran down a narrow ravine onto a flatter riverbed, which we followed for about the first 10 of the day's 33 kilometres. The problem with riverbeds is that, at some point, crossing the river becomes inevitable. In this case, we had six river crossings in the first 10 kilometres. Starting the day with wet feet is a sure-fire sign you're going to end up with blisters. I just hoped that they wouldn't be too bad. This particular riverbed was also lined with big, rough, sharp stones. More than a couple of runners came to grief on the stones and broken and twisted ankles were quite common.

Then it was up into the mountains again before we hit a long plateau. It was lovely to be running well over flat terrain, even if it was only for 11 kilometres. Just when I started to think things were going well we had another climb thrown at us and, again, there was a slide down stony dunes on the other side. Even with the tough terrain, I managed to reach the end of the stage in fourth place, which I was really happy with. I was inching myself closer and closer to a podium finish. That gave me the drive to continue, even with the shadow of the 100-kilometre day looming over me. On a stage like that, it's anyone's game—you can lose hours if you get sick or dehydrated. I tried really hard not to think about it too much, but it kept drifting to the forefront of my mind.

By the end of day three, thank goodness, the stomach problems that had been niggling away at me since Urumqi seemed to be coming right. Out in the desert, it's really hard to get your electrolyte intake exactly right and for the first couple of days mine was out of balance. With the amount that I could carry kept at a minimum, I felt hungry pretty much all the time and keeping the balance of what was going into my body in line with my energy output was not easy.

The next camp at Peach Village was a great place for us to stay overnight. We were hosted by the local people in their simple abodes. It was a great opportunity to see how people in the Gobi really live and their hospitality was really heartening. All too soon, though, day four dawned and we were back out on the trail.

It was an early start out of Peach Village, with us all back on the trail at 6.30 a.m. From the village we ran down the beautifully named Grape Valley before hitting another river-bed trail. That led us back into the huge stony sand dunes where we were running through huge steep-walled sand gullies on a single trail. The heat in these gullies was really concentrated as it was bouncing off the walls and the ground. It was a really unusual landscape to run through, too—completely unlike anything I'd seen before.

The first three days of the race hadn't been that hot. Being in the mountains the temperatures were quite mild—it was certainly much cooler at night. On day four, we started heading back down into the Turpan Depression and the temperature kept getting higher and higher. Despite the heat, I was having a really good day. I felt so good I knew I was in with a chance for a podium finish for the stage. Even knowing the next stage was the big one, and trying my best to conserve my energy for the long day, I still felt good enough to indulge in a bit of rivalry with my fellow runners.

The Singaporean runner Denvy Lo had been leading for most of the race and a bit of a rivalry had developed between the two of us. With about 3 kilometres of the stage to go, I knew Denvy was just ahead of me in second place and out in front of her was the American runner Deanna Williamson.

Going down this valley—about 3 kilometres out from the finish line—I had Denvy in my sights. I was feeling strong, so I decided, 'Right, I'm going to go for it.' She'd just passed me about an hour earlier and I knew I could take her. Even with the long day still to come, I decided I was going to have a crack at getting a stage win. The one thing that always gets me rarked up when I'm running is the Maori Battalion song. So I started to sing to myself as I ran my little heart out of my chest in that 50° heat. Echoing around the sun-baked walls of the canyon in the middle if the Gobi Desert could be heard the words of the 28th Maori Battalion marching song that so many of my people have sung to keep their spirits up in times of strife over the years:

In the days that have now gone
when the Maoris went to war
They fought until the last man died
for the honour of their tribe
And so we carry on
the conditions they have laid
And as we go on day by day
You will always hear us say
Maori Battalion march to victory
Maori Battalion staunch and true

Maori Battalion march to glory
Take the honour of the people with you
We will march, march, march to the enemy
And we'll fight right to the end.
For God! For King! And for Country!
AU—E! Ake, ake, kia kaha e!

Even with the Maori Battalion on my side, as soon as Denvy heard me behind her, she took off. She rose to the occasion and the chase was on.

The trail was so narrow that there weren't many places you could pass another runner. There were some guys plodding along in front of us, just aiming for a finish, and we were screaming at them to get out of the way. I don't think they could quite work out what was going on! Suddenly here were these two chicks racing at the end of a day in the desert. It was the stuff of legend.

I finally saw my chance and tore past her on a steep sand dune corner. My shoes were full of sand almost to bursting but there was no way I was stopping to empty them now. I knew that if I did Denvy would be straight past me again.

As I kept running, Denvy's pace fell off. I knew she'd pushed as hard as she could and didn't have anything more in the tank. I knew there was one more woman in front of me and I decided to try to chase her down as well. About 1 kilometre out from the finish line, I finally got Didi in my sights. At about the same time, a huge Buddhist temple town came into view. I knew it was the camp for the night and I had very little time to make my challenge for a stage win.

I passed her with about 600 metres to go. The guys at the finish line could see us racing and were all clapping and cheering. But I'd already spent all my energy chasing down the previous runner and I had made my move too early. With 100 metres to go, we were neck and neck but I had nothing more to give. I couldn't keep up with her. As the course went down into a dip and another sand dune rose to meet us, I couldn't hold on any longer. Didi crossed the line 50 metres and a mere 10 seconds ahead of me before we both collapsed in a heap.

The heat was brutal but we were in. I was a bit gutted because I've never actually won a stage in a race like this and I came so close that day. I was still really stoked to have come second though—I had had a really good day, and I'd done a really good time.

Once my brief celebrations were over, my thoughts turned to the poor bastards who were still out in the searing heat. The route hadn't been called the Flaming Mountains for nothing. As the afternoon wore on, the number of walking wounded making it into camp grew.

The finish was at an amazing abandoned monastery in the middle of nowhere. It was absolutely beautiful, with all these ancient sculptures still in place. But best of all, there was a river down the hill from the monastery in the base of the canyon.

After a hard day's running in extreme heat, there was only one thing for it. One of the other runners, Philippe Pech, and I walked the 800 metres down the hill. We were both covered in sand and sweat and dirt. Walking into the icy, curing, wonderful water was the best feeling I'd had in months. The purity of the water restored my tired and aching body. We stayed in the river for an hour or so and when we started to get hungry we wandered back up to the camp to get something to eat.

Unfortunately, when we got back to the camp the Chinese police who were following the race were absolutely furious that we'd been down to the river. These guys monitored our every move while we were there and they weren't happy we'd given them the slip. They told us that we were not allowed to go down to the river and threatened to close the whole race down. I couldn't believe it.

I guess it's just a sign of the nervousness that the Chinese government feel about letting a large group of foreigners run through an area of land that is close to a couple of sensitive borders and so far away from the central control of Beijing.

I felt really sorry for all of the other competitors who came in after us. There was this beautiful, cool river within walking distance but no-one else was allowed to go down there. The guards then decided to keep an even closer eye on us and insisted that all the athletes had to sleep in one big hall that night. Not ideal conditions for resting up before the 100-kilometre stage.

After our swim, we spent the rest of the afternoon waiting for the other runners to come in. By six that night, there were about twelve people who hadn't come in. Even with the extreme heat, it seemed a bit strange that so many runners were still out on the course given that it was only a 38-kilometre stage and we had started so early in the morning.

There was an air of tension in the camp. No-one was saying much but it was clear that we were all worried about our fellow competitors. Over the next wee while, the runners trickled in until there were about five of them still out on the course. Everyone was really worried. Then one of the runners came in and told us there was a guy down and unconscious about 3 kilometres back. Doctors on camels were sent out to the runner. They managed to bring him back down and get him to hospital. He was in a coma—we were all in shock and absolutely praying for him to survive. The mood at the camp was really sombre and no-one really knew what was going on.

We couldn't believe that this could have happened on a short stage. No-one had to say a word but I knew we were all thinking the same thing. How the hell were we going to survive the next day when we'd be running much further in much hotter conditions? I was frightened. I am well trained and very experienced but the situation made me aware of what can happen out there. I was scared for what I would go through and scared for the others who were slower, not so experienced and not so well trained. This was now the eve of the longest stage and we were expecting temperatures of up to 50° Celsius as we made our way through the most difficult terrain. The fear among the runners was high. What would happen tomorrow? What was happening to the runner who had collapsed? Could some of us be next? How much is too much?

The day of the Long March dawned. It was going to be 100 kilometres of absolute hell. Because of the length of the stage, runners have the choice of stopping at an overnight checkpoint for a few hours sleep in the middle of it, but I was determined to knock the beast off in one go.

I had joined forces with an Australian runner, Samantha Gash. Sam had run the Atacama Desert in South America before and she was attempting to do the four deserts in one year— the Atacama, the Gobi, the Sahara and the Antarctic. Because I had a lot of desert-running experience, she was keen to learn from me. I was looking for someone to do the long day with because I was a bit scared of doing it on my own. I've been in the desert at night before and it's not a lot of fun and games. So we decided to run together for the long day.

The next morning, everyone was still very quiet but we knew we had to focus all our energy on the day ahead. I was happy to be running with Sam—we could look after each other. Starting from the Buddhist village at 8 a.m., the first 12 kilometres were through swamps. For a desert race, the Gobi March had a surprising number of river crossings. It was a total mission to drag ourselves through these swamps and fight our way through 6-metre tall bamboo plantations. It would have been really easy to get lost.

With wet feet, the blister situation for most of us was excruciating but I had the blessing of the best pair of shoes I have ever run in, thanks to my sponsors, The North Face. Even with all the time I spent with wet feet, I never got a single blister. The North Face gear rocks.

When we finally came out of the swamp, we hit a rare piece of road. It was great to be on a road for a while and to see how local people live in the desert. From the road we veered off across sunburnt fields of nothing.

Then we hit the Turpan Depression proper. It's a massive salt lake but it was nothing like any of the other salt lakes I've run on around the world. Where they're beautiful, white, solid expanses of salt crystals, the Turpan Depression is quite muddy with a really broken-up, salt-encrusted surface. There were a few salt pools, the colour of which reminded me of the greens and oranges of the Champagne Pools in Rotorua back home.

At least there was a bit of a track through it, which made running a bit easier. Thankfully, too, there was a bit of cloud cover and the heat wasn't nearly as bad as we'd expected in the early part of the day. Sam and I really pushed ourselves to keep going while it wasn't too hot. We made sure we didn't take too many breaks. This is when training and experience can save you a lot of pain and exhaustion. Many of the slower runners and walkers don't have the option of pushing harder for a while to make it easier in total. Being slow might mean being out in the elements twice, sometimes three times, as long as the faster runners.

For mile after mile my girl Sam and I trudged our way on. We got through the 45-kilometre mark in pretty good shape. But as we ran into the evening, the heat came up all of a sudden. It got really intense really fast.

By Checkpoint Five at 55 kilometres, the casualties were mounting and even good and fast runners were going down with dehydration, electrolyte imbalance problems or dysentery. It's a fine tightrope walk trying to get the right amount of water and electrolytes and food in without overdoing the electrolytes and eating something that turns acid. The digestive system can shut down quickly so that everything you put in just fires straight back out. When we talk of dehydration, it's not a simple matter of drinking more—it doesn't work like that. Once you reach a certain point, your stomach just heaves everything back out. Thankfully, there were checkpoints about every 10 kilometres along the way and at each one all runners had to be logged in by race staff and take a minimum allocation of drinking water for the next leg. The checkpoints also provided places for runners who were struggling to rest in the shade and to seek medical advice if they needed it.

After covering 65 kilometres, we were slowing progressively. Even though we were still running it was more like a wobbly shuffling forward motion than a proper run. Sam, who is so tiny and weighs only 45 kilograms, was struggling. Our backs were bending and our eyes could only see our feet because we couldn't lift our heads anymore. At Checkpoint Six we had planned to rest for 15 minutes, but the cloud cover was gone and the humidity horrendous so I knew we would have to press on when we reached that point.

Coming out of the Turpan Depression, we came across

some irrigation streams where the locals were growing water-melons. Sam and I just fell onto the ground and stuck our heads into the water. Then we looked at each other and just cracked up laughing. There we were, laughing and crying at the same time. We were emotionally drained and slightly hys-terical as we tried to make light of this hellish situation we'd got ourselves into.

It must have looked so weird to the local villagers. It was also pretty tough being surrounded by all these lovely water-melons knowing we couldn't eat them. The Gobi March, like most of the stage races, is a self-sufficiency race. Everything you need during the day, you have to carry. Even though they looked pretty tempting, I knew that if I ate one I'd be dis-qualified from the race. There was no way I was going to risk the chance of a podium finish for a piece of fruit, no matter how tempting it looked!

After our welcome watery break, we trudged on with slightly cooled core temperatures—at least cooled enough to restore our resolve to carry on. All the gnawing doubts of the previous few kilometres were pushed to the backs of our minds again.

With the checkpoints being spaced about 10 kilometres apart, ticking each one off made us feel that much closer to finishing the stage. Unfortunately, Checkpoint Six and Check-point Seven were nearer to 16 kilometres apart than 10. It was a real mental challenge for both of us as it meant an extra hour of running before the rest and restock of water that we looked forward to checking off along the way. When we finally made it into Checkpoint Seven, we both collapsed. Sam completely let go—she was emotionally and physically exhausted. Still, after a bit of a rest and some food and drink, we both wanted to get back out on the trail. The doctors weren't keen to let

Sam go—they wanted her to rest a bit longer. After about 10 minutes, Sam started talking and joking again. I knew that as soon as she did that, she'd be fine to get moving. The medics weren't that happy about it but we had another 25 kilometres to cover and night was starting to close in. Sam and I agreed that the longer we waited the harder it would be to get back out there, so we pulled our packs back on and got back out on the trail.

As the night got darker, it became harder and harder to find the glow sticks that were supposed to be marking the route. Unsure if we were even heading in the right direction, Sam and I passed through a village. It was at this point that we got some very unwelcome company. Five men on mopeds decided to follow us along this lonely stretch of road.

It was about 11 p.m. and they rode alongside us for a good 10 kilometres. They didn't say a word. We were lost and scared. Two exhausted chicks from Downunder running around in their shorts in a remote Muslim part of China in the middle of the night was really not a good look for us.

Because we were in an area where there were villages, the kids—like kids the world over would—had taken all the signs and put them around the wrong way and moved all the ribbons marking the course. We were lost and running round in circles in the pitch dark.

I took Sam's hand and we stuck close to each other. Eventually the moped guys lost interest in us and we reached Checkpoint Eight safely. At the checkpoint, we were greeted by a Kiwi doctor, Mark Petersen. His dad, Johann, was running the race and doing extremely well. It was lovely to be met by a fellow Kiwi out in the middle of nowhere. Mark apologised for us getting lost and gave us good directions on how to get to the next checkpoint. After about five minutes at the checkpoint, we moved on. Despite Mark's instructions, we managed to get lost again and again. The dangers of running in a landscape like this at night were only too apparent, with Sam and I both managing to fall down craters, tip over banks and run around in circles.

I am not proud of it, but at one stage I started to have a panic attack when I couldn't find the way and the exhaustion was just too much. I cried and yelled abuse into the night air. Finally, I came across a volunteer who was standing out trying to find lost runners and I abused the hell out of the poor bugger! I knew it wasn't his fault but I just couldn't take it anymore. I apologised to him later for my outburst, but at the time I had been in absolute la-la land.

I was in a real panic state by this stage. Sam and I had been having alternate panic attacks and been helping each other work through them because we were starting to reach the end of our tethers. We'd been out there for 16 hours by then. We worked well as a team because she would help me and I'd help her—we'd somehow worked out subconsciously that we wouldn't both have a downer at the same time!

Having made it through the last checkpoint, we really thought we were home free. What we hadn't banked on was that the last 11 kilometres were through sand dunes. When we finally found the dunes, the battle was really on. Sam was now the stronger one and she took my hand and made me move forward. These huge dunes loomed above us and made our lives even more hellish than they had been.

It was a pitch dark night and all we had was the occasional glow stick to go by. We couldn't judge the ridges of the dunes so we just had to go up and down. We couldn't follow paths as we could have in the day time. The dunes were steep as hell and we were scrambling up them on all fours just trying to get through. We couldn't find the easiest route along the ridges so we just had to go up and down, fighting for each step. Sam and I were now both swinging between having the willpower and determination to finish and feeling as if we just couldn't do any more. I just wanted to lie down and die but Sam would pull me out of it. Then when she went down, it made me get myself together, pull her out of it and coax her on. The only good thing about it being night-time was that the temperature was more bearable.

When we finally made it over the last sand dune and heard the drum beat that signalled Camp Six—appropriately called the Oven—it felt like one of the most special moments of my life. Sam and I held hands and barrelled down the last dune towards the finish line. When we made the line, we fell over it and cried. We were both absolutely spent but relieved and happy that we'd finally made it. It was 2 a.m. and we'd been out there for 18 hours.

Our battle was over and we were second in the female race and I was about twentieth overall. I could rest and sleep now but my thoughts turned to the 150 or so poor bastards who were still out there. It would be another 18 hours before all of them had made it into camp.

The next day I slept, ate and endeavoured to endure the heat as best I could while, one by one, each battle weary runner slowly made their way into camp. There were many casualties that day—people who didn't finish the stage. My heart went out to every one of them. In my mind each one was a winner to even have come so far. In this sport, there is no shame in not making it, only in not trying. And there, but for the grace of God, go each one of us on another day.

We had done it—together Sam and I had made it.

The final stage of the race was a short 6-kilometre run into a village where we were greeted with local music, food and a party—Gobi Desert style. The first beer there went down like water. Sweaty hugs and sandy smiles were the order of the day among those of us who managed to finish the Gobi March. We had been to hell and back together. We were as close to each other as people can be because we had all done it together—each fighting our own battle and each knowing what the others had been through.

At the prize-giving I received a trophy. With a total time of 37 hours 24 minutes 26 seconds, I had come in second in the women's race. As I stood there with trophy in hand, I was shattered, tired, happy and very sad all at once. In short, I was one big emotional heap.

No-one at the prize-giving that night could celebrate fully as we all now knew what had happened to our friend and fellow runner Nicholas Kruse, who had collapsed during the fourth stage. Taking part in this kind of race, we all understood that there is some risk involved, but nothing can prepare you for losing one of your fellow runners. At just 31 years old, Nick had passed away. Hailing from the United States, he had been living and working in Shanghai for a number of years and had always dreamed of running through the Gobi Desert. He achieved his dream but, sadly, it proved fatal for him.

Not long before he collapsed during the fourth stage of the race, Nick had been seen by Mark Petersen, the Kiwi medic who had been so kind to Sam and I on the Long March. Mark had stopped and had a chat with Nick and reported that he had been in good spirits and didn't seem to be in any apparent difficulty.

It wasn't long after that when another competitor came across Nick collapsed on the course just 1.5 kilometres from the finish line of the fourth stage. That runner stayed with him until two more athletes arrived who ran on to camp to alert officials. An ambulance was called to evacuate Nick, who was suffering from severe heat stroke. While the ambulance was en route, a medic from the camp headed up to where Nick was and administered intravenous fluids in the field until evacuation could be completed. The part of the course where he had collapsed was not accessible by vehicle and Nick had to be evacuated by camel.

About an hour and a half after he was found, Nick was transferred to an ambulance and taken to Turpan Hospital nearby. Once there, he was stabilised and transferred to Urumqi Hospital. An event doctor stayed with Nicholas while he was at the hospital. She reported that he was receiving excellent care, and that his condition was stable but critical.

Two days later, on Saturday, 3 July, while preparations were being made in discussion with his family to transfer Nick to Hong Kong, his condition worsened. He passed away at 5.30 p.m. with his girlfriend and brother by his side.

Nick's death was a tragedy that touched every runner and official involved with the Gobi March that year. His memory will be held close by each and every one of us.

Ultra-race gear list

For a self-supported race like the Gobi March, the organisers are very strict about what you can and cannot take with you on the course. At the pre-race briefing all gear is inspected to ensure that every athlete is playing by the rules. This is a typical gear list for a race like this:

Compulsory equipment
Backpack/rucksack
Sleeping bag
Headlamp and back-up light
Compass
Safety pins
Knife/multitool—like a Swiss Army knife
Whistle
Survival blanket
Sunscreen
Lip sunscreen
Blister kit
Medication
Alcohol gel
Toilet paper/wet wipes
Red flashing light
Compression bandage

Compulsory clothing
Lightweight jacket
Shorts/tights
T-shirts
Shoes
Socks
Headgear/cap

Warm hat
Sunglasses
Nationality patches

Compulsory seven-day food supply
Dried meals
Energy gels/bars
Nutrition supplements
Coffee/tea/hot chocolate
Snacks
Eating utensil
Electrolytes
Hydration system

Optional equipment
Sleeping pad
Bag liner
Trekking poles
Insect repellent
Waterproof/sandproof bags
Towel
Toothbrush/toothpaste
Wristwatch
GPS
iPod
Portable solar charger
Camera
Book/magazine
Training books/maps

Optional clothing
Gloves
Scarf/headgear

Gaiters

Flip flops/slippers

Sports bra (women only)

Optional food/cooking

Eating tin/cup

Lisa's advice on acclimatising to heat

Many of the world's best known ultras are held in deserts—think Badwater, the Marathon des Sables in Morocco, Raid Sahara in Egypt, and three of the Racing the Planet 4 Deserts Series, the Gobi, the Sahara and the Atacama (the fourth desert being Antarctica). Acclimatising to the heat before you run these races is absolutely vital, especially for someone like me who lives in a place where the climate is temperate at best, and downright cold at worst.

For each of my Badwater races, from midwinter temperatures in New Plymouth of around 5–10° Celsius I was thrust into 48–57° Celsius. My first few days acclimatising in the Arizona desert were absolutely painful and pretty disheartening. I could barely handle running without being totally exhausted and needing to sleep straight afterwards. But day by day, I increased the amount of training I was doing by 20 or 30 minutes until I was running two and a half hours in the heat quite comfortably. I then tapered back down to recover before the start of the race. It took ten days, but I eventually acclimatised for the horrendous conditions that lay ahead of me in Death Valley.

Heat can be lethal—it must be taken seriously. I have been in a race where someone young, fit and healthy died from heat-related difficulties. I have also seen a number of people suffer from kidney failure because they were insufficiently prepared for the toll that the moisture loss caused by heat can take on the body.

My advice for anyone who wants to run in desert heat is that it's essential you acclimatise your body to desert conditions as much as possible. It takes about 10 days to do this so try to spend at least that amount of time in, or as close as possible to, the race environment.

If you are unable to spend that long at the race location, try to replicate the conditions at home in the four weeks leading up to the event. One way of doing this is to use a sauna. Starting three weeks out from the event, spend fifteen minutes a day in the sauna. Then gradually increase the time spent so that just before you leave for the race it's up to around 45 minutes a day. It is critical that you increase your intake of both fluids and electrolytes over this time.

Just remember that saunas count as part of your training and they will fatigue you just as much as a training run will. It's a good idea to have a sauna after you've been out running and not before. Exercising in the sauna can help, too, but make sure you don't overdo it.

Another risk of acclimatising this way is the possibility of catching a cold when you come out of the sauna. To minimise this risk, always take a cold shower to close your pores when you come out of the sauna. It's also a good idea to increase your intake of vitamin C over this time. If you decide to take a vitamin C supplement, make sure it's a bio-available one.

A more simple method of heat acclimatisation is to layer up your clothes. Pile on thermals and fleeces then go out running in the middle of the day. It's a really unpleasant way to train but it is really effective as it mimics the humid conditions that you'll experience in a hot environment.

5

Return to the Sahara

You get on the road and the whistle blows and you're off. For however long you're racing, there's nothing else in your mind but surviving to make it to the finish line.

4 Deserts Sahara Race, 3–9/10/2010

After my experience in the Gobi, I knew I couldn't stay away from the desert for very long. For me, there's nothing that compares to doing these long, self-supported races. And when it comes to desert running, the Sahara keeps drawing me back time and time again. So it was that I entered the Sahara Race organised by 4 Deserts, the same outfit who managed the Gobi March.

I know I keep saying that you need six months recuperation after a big race but once again I went against my own advice. Just three months after my race in the Gobi, I was en route to the Sahara once again. This time the race was being held in Egypt, in the desert south-west of Cairo.

My first mission in the Sahara was a mad mission through the Libyan Desert. A bunch of us had gone out there with only what we could carry and no-one really knew where we were. It was a miracle that we all survived it, but what I learned on that trek has stood me in good stead ever since. Besides which, after that mission, a seven-day 250-kilometre race with checkpoints every 10 kilometres providing water seems a whole lot easier to me than it might to other people.

Making this race extra special was the fact that my mate Megan, who had crewed for me at Death Valley and on the NZ Run, was coming with me. This time, she wasn't there to support me—she was going to be running the whole thing herself!

Megan hadn't really done any running until she started crewing for me. Then, she was so preoccupied with running alongside me and helping me get through, she ran distances she never thought she was capable of. When she added up how many hundreds of kilometres she'd actually run, she realised she was a runner after all. I saw real physical changes in Megan after that as she started really training. Then I said, 'I'm going to the Sahara, do you want to come?' I believed she could do it. She didn't think she could, but she agreed anyway.

For someone who never wanted to leave the country, I was pretty impressed when she went off to the Sahara on her own and spent two weeks travelling through Egypt by herself before the race. I wouldn't do that! In fact, while Megan was wandering around Egypt, I was spending time in Paris. It's not the ideal place to acclimatise to desert conditions, but it did give me a chance to get over my jet lag before hitting the heat of the Sahara. My decision to spend time in Paris instead of Cairo was, in part, influenced by the trouble I had with my tummy in Urumqi before the Gobi March. This time, I didn't want to risk getting a dodgy stomach in Cairo before the race started.

It's amazing where running can take you: before heading across the sands of the Sahara and finishing outside the pyramids of Giza I got to visit the most romantic city in Europe. In Paris I met up with Philippe Pech, one of the ultrarunners I'd met during the Gobi. For the first couple of days I had a bit of trouble adjusting my body clock and, for some reason, my asthma was quite bad. That said, I'm pretty sure it would have been much worse in Cairo.

Hanging out with Philippe was great—he made sure that I trained while I was there. It was quite a mad experience doing a training run that passed through downtown Paris, along the River Seine, past the Louvre down to Notre Dame, up to the Eiffel Tower and through some of Paris's elegant shopping areas. The pair of us didn't really fit in among all the big-brand shops and beautifully dressed people.

I had hoped it would be a bit warmer in Paris than it was. Most of the time I was there, the temperature hardly got above 12°—not ideal for transitioning into the 40°+ I was expecting in the Sahara.

From Paris I flew to Cairo where, thankfully, Megan was waiting to meet me at the airport. I was bloody glad to see her as I knew that Cairo could be a scary adventure in itself. The pair of us headed back to her hotel for the night.

I woke the next morning with a big ugly cold sore and feeling unfit and nervous. To top that off, I also had a wee bit of asthma. I've come to realise it's a fairly standard panic reaction of mine—it's my body talking to me. It's saying, 'Aaarrgh! For goodness sake don't do it to me again . . . ' Times like that, my head just has to tell my body to shut up, toughen up and get on with the job.

•

It never ceases to amaze me how my body tries to cause problems just before a race. It's a psychological thing—it's as if my fear is trying to stop me from achieving my goals. All I can do is take a deep breath and ignore it. Luckily, I didn't really have long to dwell on feeling a bit crook that morning—we had to be at competitor registration quite early.

At registration, we were given a competitor briefing, and then our gear was checked to make sure we had all of the compulsory equipment required in the race rules. It's really important to make sure you have it all at check-in because if you're missing anything the race organisers can give you a time penalty for each missing item or, in extreme cases, not allow you to start the race.

One of the things that the organisers always check carefully is the food that you're carrying. In your pack, there must be enough food for seven days. But the rules are even more specific than that. The food that you're carrying must total enough for you to take in 8400 kilojoules per day for the duration of the race.

At the check-in, medical staff are also on hand to ensure that all the competitors are fit enough to take part in the race. The decision as to whether you're allowed to start the race, or not, will sometimes come down to them.

Having breezed through registration and our equipment check, around 200 of us mad runners from more than 40 countries all climbed onto buses and headed deep into the desert, to spend the night together near the starting point of the race. It was good to catch up with some of the guys I'd run with in other races. Ricky Paugh, Sam Gash and Jack Denness were all there and ready to go again. Sahara here we come, two Taranaki girls heading out . . .

Unlike the Gobi, I had a good idea of the type of conditions we were likely to encounter in the Sahara. This is exactly the kind of landscape most people think of when they think of the desert. There are huge mountains of rock, surrounded by the most golden dunes of sand imaginable, and if you're lucky, you'll also come across the odd desert oasis complete with fresh water and palm trees. The temperatures out there are likely to reach 50° Celsius at the height of the day before dropping considerably at night. As usual, I was hoping I wouldn't have to spend too much time running at night as the reflective nature of sand makes it really hard to work out your footing in the dark. Only time would tell just how long my long days would be.

We finally arrived at the first camp, beside Lake Al Fayyum, late that evening. It was quite a cool setting for a camp—right near the road and quite close to civilisation. That's kind of unusual for a race like this but, as usual, everyone was pretty nervous knowing the next morning we'd all be off into the desert again.

The Sahara Race takes pretty much the same form as the Gobi March. There are four 'short' days that cover approximately 40 kilometres each, then there's the Long March—in this case it was going to be 95 kilometres—then the final day is shorter—this time it was going to be a 10-kilometre day.

It didn't take long before I realised how silly it was to not have spent more time in Egypt before the race. From quite early on the first day I was really struggling. The wind was really extreme. The route took us around the lake. It's a salt-water lake so nothing like the fresh water oases you expect to see out in the desert. The landscape around it was quite barren except for a few scrubby bushes. You'd think that running around water would make the temperatures a bit more bearable but the opposite was true. In the desert, the heat is usually very dry. But around the lake there was quite a bit of humidity that, combined with windy conditions, made for uncomfortable running.

Quite early in the day, I teamed up with an Australian runner called Malcolm Brown. I'd met Malcolm in the Gobi Desert and it was good to catch up with him again. He's a much stronger runner than me but he was struggling a bit, too, so we hung out together for a while. It was nice to have someone I knew to run with for a while.

The course was quite flat but the wind was crazy. This time, I found the Sahara really hot and dry. I know that sounds stupid, given I was running in the world's largest non-polar desert, but the other times I'd run there I hadn't got nearly as burnt or dried out by the wind. The sunburn and wind chaffing were horrendous this time.

Getting away from the lake, the humidity dropped a bit, which made running easier on my lungs but it wasn't long before my back started to hurt and I was really starting to feel the effects of sunburn and wind chaffing. At the end of the day, I got to the camp in reasonably good shape. Once in, I was gutted to hear that Jack Denness, who I'd known since the first time I'd run in Death Valley, had had problems with his kidneys that day and ended up in hospital in Cairo. Jack is an absolute legend of the sport. He holds the record for being the oldest runner to complete Badwater—at the age of 75—in what was his twelfth time running Death Valley.

Because we weren't that far from civilisation, there were reports of women in the race being attacked by local men. It turned out that six female runners were harassed during the first day. In one case, a man jumped out of some bushes on the edge of the lake and grabbed one of the runners, who managed to get away, but she was badly shaken. She ran on alone and terrified to the next checkpoint. I was impressed with the race organisers on this occasion. They gathered her up and took her back to base for a check-up then allowed her to continue the race. Usually, if you leave the race for any reason you are automatically disqualified. In this case, I believe the organisers, by making an exception, did absolutely the right thing by this particular athlete.

At the briefing in camp that night, the organisers asked the guys in the race to try to keep an eye out for the female runners and, where possible, to team up and run with them. The presence of a male runner would always deter these opportunistic perverts who saw the female runners as being fair game because they were women on their own.

In these self-supporting races, who your tent-mates are can make a huge difference to how you cope during the race. If you get a great bunch of tent-mates, you can often end up looking out for each other and developing a real sense of camaraderie.

In the Sahara, there were eight of us to a tent. The tent allocations are made randomly but you can specify other runners that you want to tent with. Naturally, I was sharing my tent with Megan but the rest of our tent-mates were decided by process of a lucky dip. We were really lucky in that we had two German runners in our tent. One of them, Volker Voss, was 68 years old and the spitting image of Omar Sharif. He seriously looked like he'd just stepped out of Lawrence of Arabia. He was a real character and it was inspiring to see someone still out there kicking arse at his age. The second German in our tent, Rafael Fuchsgruber, ended up being one of the top runners in the race. He was an awesome athlete and, as always at an event like this, spending time with the elite runners I learned a lot.

On the downside, in our tent we had a runner who shall remain nameless—the loudest snorer I think I've ever heard. It was horrendous. It was bad enough that I was sleeping on the ground in an open tent in the middle of nowhere surrounded by flies. Having to put up with a tent-mate who sounded like a freight train made it even worse. Worse still was knowing that it was just the first night of six that I'd have to spend listening to that racket.

Half the tent got up and went outside to sleep just to get away from it. I couldn't help but think that he should have gone outside to sleep but he didn't give a shit—after all he was getting a good night's sleep. When you're in such close quarters with a lot of strangers, other people's funny little habits really get up your nose quite quickly. Old snorey chops was sleeping next to me and at one point I decided there was nothing for it but to hit him to try and wake him up. The others were trying to kick his feet but he took no notice whatsoever.

It wasn't all bad though—it was great to be sharing my tent with Megan. She was really happy to be out there and, in some ways, she was in better shape than I was. I think I was still quite tired from the Gobi and I was mentally a bit down. Not having had time to adjust to the heat or the time difference was taking its toll on me.

For part of the second day we were followed by a documentary team making a movie called *Desert Runners*, profiling six ultramarathon runners. I had gotten to know them in the Gobi and they'd selected me as one of the runners to be in the movie. It was quite an honour to be included along with Sam Gash, Ricky Paugh from the United States, Dave O'Brien from Ireland, and Tremaine Kent and Phil Tye from the United Kingdom.

The documentary crew interviewed us as we were running,

which was quite a good distraction but it was sometimes quite hard to concentrate on running and sounding intelligent at the same time. Jennifer Steinman, the film's director and producer, and Sevan Matossian, the director of photography, were really thorough and spent plenty of time running alongside us. To ensure that they got the fullest picture possible of what we do as ultrarunners, they interviewed us before, during and after each stage.

Most of the day consisted of going up and down massive sand dunes that often had a kind of plateau at the top of them. Running on sand dunes is quite tricky as you spend a lot of time picking around trying to find the best track. Climbing the dunes, you have to track along the side of the dune rather than running straight up it. You have one foot higher than the other the whole way and you're slipping and sliding running along the side of the dune.

For a good portion of the day I ran with Sam, but I really struggled to keep up with her and her crew. I did my best, but at the top of one of the dunes I lost them. I just couldn't maintain the kind of pace that they were doing because my back had started to pack up on me. Even though my pack was only 10 kilograms, it might as well have been 100 for the pain it was causing me.

It had been a long time since I'd experienced back pain like I did in the Sahara. Every time I slipped on one of the dunes my back would go into massive painful nerve spasms that would drop me to my knees. I started to really worry that if one of the spasms stayed I wouldn't be able to move at all. Thankfully, that didn't happen.

At the top of the dunes there was usually a harder, stony table-top bit. It was always a relief to not only get to the top but also to set foot on more solid ground. The views from

Chris Cruikshank and I during the 2009 Badwater Ultramarathon.

My top crew. From left: race director Chris Kostman, naming rights sponsor Murray Dick, Casey Potatau, Chris Cruikshank, Megan Stewart, paramedic and sponsor, and sponsors Jason Mumby and the legend Howard Dell.

With schoolkids doing the 'K Per Day Challenge' during the NZ run.

Cape Reinga. A bloody long way from Bluff, but not the end of the journey.

My family is my rock. From left to right: Dawson, my dad Cyril, my mum Isobel and Mitchell. My biggest supporters were at the finish line of the NZ Run, at the Hilton Hotel near Viaduct Harbour, Auckland.

The Gobi March, during the 12-kilometre-long riverbed running section on day three.

With my international friends Philippe Pech, left, and Ahn, right, in the Gobi.

Sam Gash and I on the day of the Long March during the Sahara Race. (Image © Jennifer Steinman)

At the finish line of the Sahara Race, in front of the Pyramids of Giza in Cairo. (Image © Jennifer Steinman)

On the trail during The North Face 100 race in the Blue Mountains.

The North Face photo shoot in the Blue Mountains, before the fateful ripped ankle. (Image © Mark Watson, courtesy of The North Face)

Inside the Hypoxico Altitude Training tent, the at-home training system that ended in disaster. (Image courtesy of the *Taranaki Daily News*)

Training before La Ultra The High on Khardung La, one of the highest motorable pass in the world, in the Kashmir region of the Himalayas, India. (Image © Chris Ord)

Tanglang La in a snow storm. I'd been on the road for about 45 hours at this stage: long, lonely miles. (Image © Chris Ord)

At the finish line of La Ultra The High after 222 kilometres. Left to right: Venkat Krishnan, Josh Paurini, Chris Ord, Ranjit Singh and the camp doctor.

Training up on Mt Taranaki in the rain. (Image courtesy of the *Taranaki Daily News*)

the top of the dunes were absolutely unbelievable. Not that I spent much time up there taking them in. The wide open expanses made me feel like an ant crawling through the sand.

Coming down after Checkpoint Three of that day, I was running flat stick down this massive sand dune. It was the best feeling. My shoes were full of sand but I was so happy to be on my way down, I just didn't care. As I ran down, I came alongside a Korean guy. Neither of us could speak each other's languages but it didn't matter. We were both having such a good time that we didn't need to have words to communicate how happy we both were. You quite often have experiences like that in races like this. It doesn't matter if you don't share a common language with other runners because we all understand what the others are going through.

After hurtling down that dune, it was back to climbing again. The camp was halfway up the next mountain and I was really glad to finally reach it. By the time I got to camp, my back was a raw mess from the straps on my backpack cutting into it. I've always had trouble with backpacks damaging my back. In fact, my back is so scarred that I recently got a traditional ta moko tattoo on it to cover all my backpack battle scars. The tattoo represents my family, my tribal affiliations, and all the adventures that I've had. It was really painful but nowhere near as painful as getting the scars in the first place.

That night I went to the medics and they padded my whole back with this really thick padding. I kept it on for the rest of the race and getting it off after the race was a real mission. Between my back and Megan's manky blistered feet we were a pretty sorry pair. To make things a little bit better, the sunset that night was absolutely brilliant—almost enough to cheer us up.

The third day was really tough for me again. Right from

the beginning, it was up and down the whole way. All the other runners tore off at a hell of a pace and because I always go out slowly, I got left behind quite quickly. I was struggling with my breathing a bit because I really don't cope with undulating terrain. The constant change of heart rate that constant climbing and then descending requires really challenges me. It also usually causes me to have asthma attacks.

I was well behind Sam at this stage and we were vying for fourth and fifth place at the time. Ahead of us were Katia Figini from Italy, Hadley Lund from the US and Michelle Pude from Australia. They were a way ahead of us so there was a bit of rivalry between me and Sam. Originally we'd planned to run the whole race together but she ended up running with the guys from her tent because they were in better form than me.

At one point during the day I ran past Jacqueline Terto from Brazil. She didn't speak any English and I don't speak Portuguese but we were both really struggling in the heat of the day. It was 40°+ and the heat was just banging down on us. Throughout the day we kept passing each other but we encouraged each other to keep going. At one stage, she reached across and took my hand. We ran together hand in hand for a little while. That kind of human action can really make the difference to your race when you're in a world of pain. The pair of us would chat away in our own languages but the real encouragement was in the pats on the shoulders and the smiles that we shared.

After a while, we were climbing another massive table-top mountain and she dropped off behind me. There was a checkpoint at the top of the mountain and I could see the final camp from there. It looked really close but in the desert distances are hard to work out. The camp looked like it was just down the hill and along a flat bit and then I'd be there. Three hours later I was still running and it didn't seem to be any closer. As I was running down the hill towards the camp, I got my period. Who'd want to be a girl in the middle of the desert? There was no way I was going to stop this close to the end of the day so I ran along stuffing toilet paper down my pants. There's no dignity in the desert, that's for sure.

When I got to the checkpoint, Sam had beaten me in by about 20 minutes. Every night in camp I tried to update my blog to let my family and friends know I was still alive and still moving. Sitting in the computer tent was horrible. It was always really hot and full of flies, but it seems a bit wrong to complain when having contact with the outside world from the middle of the desert really is a luxury—even when the satellite link-up doesn't seem to work very well.

Day four was pretty much a carbon copy of the previous day. I spent most of the day trailing Sam up and down sand dunes, doing battle with my back and worrying about how I was going to manage to complete the Long March coming up.

That night, I watched a young English woman, Emma Fergusson, come into camp. She was in such bad shape, I couldn't even begin to imagine how she'd get through the next day. She could barely get from one end of the camp to the other. It took her half an hour to cross that short distance her feet were so bad. I didn't think there was any way she'd make it but she did. She didn't look like your typical athlete but she's one of the most gutsy people I've ever met. You can never judge an athlete by the way they look. It's all about what's on the inside—it's about heart and determination.

At the end of day four, my own body was in pretty rough condition. I'd pretty much lost all my toenails and my feet were badly blistered. But it was my back that was really giving me the most grief. The straps of my backpack had cut into my shoulders causing open wounds. Every time I tried to bend down or adjust my pack, my sciatic nerve would cause paralysing pain in my back. Usually I can work through these kind of problems but this time I found it particularly hard to get past the pain. Three years of full-on racing were really starting to take their toll on me.

All I could think in camp that night was that I was due for a holiday. And the next day was going to be anything but a rest. I spent the whole night trying to get my head in a better space as I knew that my mental toughness was going to be the only thing that would get me through what was looming ahead—the Long March.

It's not surprising I was scared silly at the prospect of running a 95-kilometre stage in 50° heat. My broken-down body and my heavy pack meant the next day would be hard going. But around the campfire at Camp Four the camaraderie among the runners gave me a really good boost. Also helping my state of mind as I thought about the next day was knowing that I'd be running with my old mate from the Gobi, Sam Gash.

Sharing Sam's tent were a couple of Irish guys, Maghnus Collins-Smyth and David Burns. These two were best mates and had had some pretty crazy adventures together. They'd not long got back from completing an epic bike ride from Cape Town in South Africa back to their home in Ireland. They'd cycled some 18,000 kilometres through some of the roughest, poorest, hottest and most dangerous countries on the planet.

Along the way they met up with Alistair Humphries, who is one of only a handful of people to have cycled around the earth. Alistair mentioned to the two Irishmen that he'd run the Marathon des Sables race in the Moroccan Sahara. When Humphries said it was the hardest thing he'd ever done, Maghnus decided he'd have to give this desert running a crack, which is how he and Dave found themselves out here in the middle of nowhere with me and Sam.

Maghnus had run his first marathon three weeks prior to coming to Egypt and then a week after that he injured his knee and had to stop training. I did wonder a little bit what we were letting ourselves in for joining forces with these two, but when Maghnus told me that he'd broken three vertebrae in his back and had come back from that injury to be here, I felt a certain kinship with him. When I was in my early twenties, I'd sustained a similar injury falling off a flying fox. I was told I'd never run again but I proved those doctors wrong. I knew the determination it took to get over an injury like that. I really believe that sometimes a strong determination and ability to put up with a lot of discomfort and pain and a passionate attitude to adventure are more important prerequisites for this sort of undertaking than any amount of training.

Sam and I had always planned to do the long stage together after our successful teamwork in the Gobi Desert. The addition of the boys to our running group came as a result of their concern for the women in the race. After what had happened on the first day, with a number of female runners being harassed by local men, quite a few of the guys were very conscious of keeping an eye on the female athletes in the race to make sure nothing like that happened again. It's that kind of selflessness that makes me really appreciate the kind of people this sport attracts.

When the long day finally started, I awoke at 4.30 a.m. to the sounds of other runners rustling about getting ready. I had that sinking feeling in the pit of my stomach when I realised where I was and what lay ahead that day. I rolled over and tried to ignore the noises for a few precious moments of quiet.

I had had my feet up on a cardboard box half the night trying to release the nerve pain in my back. I said a wee silent prayer that my back and, indeed, my body would hold together for me one more time. I took a deep breath and steeled myself, knowing it would be a long time before I would lie down again. I could feel my enthusiasm waning at the prospect of what lay ahead, and I just hoped that I would be able to keep up with Sam and the Irish lads because the thought of being out in the desert by myself at night terrified me.

At 6 a.m. all of the athletes attended a camp briefing. There we were given a little info about what to expect—the difficult passages, the distance between checkpoints, some of the key markers on the way, and information about where to get medical help if we needed it.

As is usual on the morning of a long stage, all the competitors were more subdued than usual. Many were already walking wounded, like Megan and her horribly blistered feet. For some—like Megan, Maghnus and Dave—it was their first time doing this sort of crazy distance. The more experienced among us—like Sam and me—might seem to have it easier, but we know the hell that we are in for and that can have a negative effect on your psyche.

On the previous day, Dave's knee had given him a lot of grief and then, somehow, came right again. Sam's knee had also been giving her niggles. My back was buggered, with the nerve pain still occasionally becoming so paralysing that it dropped me to my knees. Maghnus was crossing his fingers, too, that his back would hold up. What a great bunch we were.

We were told to expect a lot of sand dunes, but we were also promised it would be spectacular. Dunes are hard going to climb but bloody great to run down the other side of. We would also be passing through the famous open-air museum known as the Valley of the Whales, or Wadi el-Hitan. Apparently, you can see 40-million-year-old whale fossils in the area. It's a real tourist attraction with visitors making the trek from hundreds of kilometres away to see these wonders. It seems unimaginable that all those years ago, the Sahara was underwater.

At 6.30 a.m., when the gun went off, the four of us took off at a fast pace—too fast probably. I slotted in behind Sam and the boys and just tried to hang in there. The field quickly dissipated and we were down to around seven runners in a loose bunch, mostly people from Sam's tent. The sand was soft and the landscape undulating to start. We had vehicle tracks to follow here and we criss-crossed them trying to find the easiest or most hard-packed part to run on. The track was constantly changing and we had to keep our eyes peeled for the best spot. Whenever one of us found a good hard bit, we'd call out to the others and we'd all fall into a line, swerving in and out, close together then apart, one leading then another. We must have looked a bit like the lead bunch in the Tour de France.

The first 20 kilometres went by pretty much like that. No-one had much to say and we just all kept running together, looking out for each other and getting into a bit of a rhythm for the day. The first couple of checkpoints we didn't really even stop. At each checkpoint, every runner is recorded as having been through. Rather than line up to get our numbers ticked off, we'd just yell them to the volunteers then go and refill our water bottles before getting back out onto the course.

The less time spent at these checkpoints, the better. We all knew that as the day wore on the heat would become more intense so we wanted to get as many kilometres out of the way as we could before it got too hot. As predicted, the heat came in with a vengeance at about 10 a.m. and didn't cool down until the sun went down much later. As it got hotter, we all began to suffer a little more but we kept on running.

Checkpoint Three was at the Valley of the Whales. We all knew that this was a 'once in a lifetime' opportunity to see fossilised whales in the middle of the desert, but we also knew that whatever time we spent looking at them was more valuable minutes that we'd have to spend out in the sun. I also knew that lifting my head to look at the skeletons would really bloody hurt so there was no way I was doing it. So I can say I've visited the Valley of the Whales, but I never actually saw a whale.

It was not long after the third checkpoint that Dave started to have real trouble with his knee. Sam and I kept running, while Maghnus was spending quite a bit of time running with us and then dropping back to see if Burnsey was OK. We all hoped that his knee would come right the way it had the previous day but it was not to be.

Coming out of Checkpoint Four, Dave's knee locked up completely. Sam and I didn't realise he was having as much trouble as he was and we raced through the checkpoint as usual. Straight out of the checkpoint there was a really huge sand dune and the pair of us powered our way up to the top of it as best we could. Ordinarily I probably would have marvelled at how spectacular the view was but with the heat and the pain in my back I was just focused on putting one foot in front of the other and getting back down the other side.

Eventually Maghnus caught up with us but Dave was nowhere to be seen. Ever the gentleman, Maghnus headed back to the checkpoint to find out what was happening with his mate. At this point, Sam and I thought we might have lost the lads altogether. They'd done so much together it seemed unlikely that they'd split up now.

We were pretty surprised when Maghnus caught up with us about 2 kilometres later. He told us that Dave had decided to walk the rest of the stage and they'd agreed that Maghnus should go ahead and run it at his own pace. I could tell from Maghnus's expression that he'd really struggled having to make the decision to leave his best mate behind. I felt bad for Dave but I was glad that we'd have our protector alongside us going into the night part of the race.

Sometime between Checkpoints Four and Five, another Irish guy started running with us. It was kind of weird because he stayed about 50 metres ahead of us or 50 metres behind us, using our little group as pacemakers. The strange thing was he never introduced himself or indeed said a word to us. As we ran, Sam, Maghnus and I would share food, chat to each other and help each other out. Not this guy. He was like a weird shadow—he added nothing to our experience of the race.

It was around about the halfway mark that Sam had a wee meltdown. Usually tough as nails, Sam started to cry. When we asked her what was up, she told us that her grandmother had just visited her and was here to help her. She then went on to tell us that her grandmother had died just before she left to come to Egypt. I wasn't quite sure what to say but the reassurance that her grandmother was there with her really gave Sam a boost to keep going.

Coming in to Checkpoint Five, our nameless silent Irish shadow did something that became his pattern for the rest of the race. Just as we neared the checkpoint, he ran ahead to make sure that he was counted first in the rankings. It really annoyed the three of us and gave us something to talk about for a while.

After Checkpoint Five, Maghnus hit a bit of a downer. I could tell his back was killing him and mine was not much better. He'd been on his feet longer than he'd ever been in his life and still had so far to go. I tried to help him snap out of his low by asking him what motivated him to keep going. He said, 'You realise pretty soon that you really couldn't give a shit what other people think. That's not what motivates me, and I am not motivated by a desire to win, which is good as that's not likely to happen anytime soon. I am just here to prove something to myself, and I want to know that I have given it a hundred per cent. You know you can get through something like this with just 50 per cent and everyone else will still think the same of you but you can't fool yourself.'

We'd planned to stop at Checkpoint Six for something to eat. All of the checkpoints have hot water so you can cook up your dehydrated meals. The plan had been to stop, rehydrate our food and take time out to eat it. But we got to the check-point quite early and agreed that we should keep running while there was still light. Racing through the checkpoint, we filled out water bottles and poured the water into our dehy-drated meals and kept running. We ate and ran, sharing the meals as we went. The pressure was really on. Up and down sand dunes, the three of us just kept on running, shuffling, sliding . . . whatever we could do to keep moving forward.

With our plans of stopping at Checkpoint Six out the win-dow, we just carried on. As it turned out, we didn't stop at the next two checkpoints either. In part it was because we wanted to get a good time for the stage and, in part, for me anyway, it was because the way my back was hurting, I wasn't sure I'd be able to start again if I stopped.

Even though Maghnus was battling with his own back pain, he'd always be there to help me or Sam if we got into difficulty. We'd be running up a sand dune and if he'd realise I was struggling he'd pull me up the last few metres. When we got to the second-to-last checkpoint, I was in such a bad way that I couldn't even bend down to take the sand out of my shoes. Maghnus got down on his hands and knees and changed my shoes for me. It was a huge thing for him to do for me, especially when he was exhausted, too. I really believe that it's that kind of action that tells you so much about a person's character.

Speaking of being able to tell a lot about a person, our silent Irish mate stayed with us until just after the final checkpoint. With about 10 kilometres left to go, he bolted off into the night. Pretty much as soon as he knew he would be all right, he decided to make a dash to the finish line. We were all pretty pissed off with him by this point. He really used us for his own benefit without a thought for any of us. It leaves a really bad taste in your mouth. We'd done all the hard yards pacing for him and he didn't share a thing with us. I guess this sort of racing can bring out the best and the worst in people. And it doesn't matter where you are or what you're doing, there are always going to be selfish bastards who only care about winning.

The one good thing about this bloke shadowing us was that it gave us something to talk about and it took our mind off our various ailments. Before we knew it, the finish line was in sight. We'd been to hell and stayed there for a long time. We'd pushed our speed as much as we could and we'd taken no breaks. Brave, or crazy? Whichever we were, we'd done it.

It was about 9.45 at night when we finished and we'd been through a 15 hour and 15 minute battle—me, Sam and Maghnus. Just as we were crossing the finish line we saw a meteor flash across the sky. We just looked at each other and were like, 'This had to be!' It was amazing. There were hugs and tears of relief at being able to stop moving forward and stop pushing and driving and forcing ourselves to move.

Despite all the trouble he'd had with his knee, Burnsey showed incredible determination to finish the long day just two hours behind the three of us. Those Irish rugby boys have got some real grit.

Once I'd recuperated a bit from our ordeal, my thoughts turned to my good mate, Megan, who was still out there in the desert. She was about 30 kilometres behind and still had all these battles ahead. I knew it would be a while before she made it back to camp so went to our tent and had a bit of a sleep. I woke at about 5 or 6 a.m. I hadn't slept that well because there were runners coming in all night. Every time someone crossed the finish line there were drummers playing to welcome them in. That's great if you're the runner, but not so great if you're trying to sleep! Every time I woke up, I'd think, 'Where's Megan? Is she all right? Have I killed my best mate?' I worked out that she'd be in about six-ish so I got up. And she didn't come. And she didn't come. There were heaps of other runners finishing and the longer it took, the more worried I got.

As the morning wore on, the heat just grew more intense. The hotter it got, the more I worried. I knew she'd been out there for more than 24 hours, which is a bloody long time. I seriously started to wonder whether she was going to make it. It wasn't until 10 a.m. that I finally, finally saw this familiar figure in the distance wobbling along. I raced over to the finish line and I was so stoked. She crawled over the line and her first words were, 'Lisa, I've never been so fucked in all my life.'

I took her backpack off her and poured water over her to

cool her down. Once you've finished the race you still have to get across the compound to reach the camp. It might not seem that far but when you've just done 100 kilometres it seems like miles. I was telling her that she needed to get rehydrated and get her feet looked at. She got to the tent and she just crumpled to her knees and collapsed on her face. She was lying across the tent—a small tent for eight people and she was comaed-out in the middle of it. I checked her pulse and left her sleeping where she fell. We all tiptoed around her but when it got to six hours I started to worry a bit. I knew she should have rehydrated before she went to sleep but she was having none of it.

We moved her out of the middle of the tent and she still didn't wake up. It was boiling hot in the tent and I realised that I had to wake her up. It was about four in the afternoon before I finally managed to wake her and she was a little bit sick. I got the fluids back into her and, even though she was knackered and sick and her feet were manky, she was stoked. She looked at me and just said, 'I did it!'

Everybody was in from the long race day in the Sahara. We were all chatting away, all happy because we'd done it and we just had the short run around the pyramids the next day. Then we heard the drums start up again. The drums always meant that someone was coming. It had been a few hours since the last runner had come in. We'd checked in on all the people who had come in late, because we knew they'd been to hell and back. We thought everyone was either back or out of the race. When the drums started again, I thought, 'You've got to be kidding me.' We were sitting out in the baking sun and I realised that some bastard was still out there.

The whole camp went across to the finish line. The music was playing and we watched this Korean guy inching his way across the last kilometre to the line. It took forever for him to come across the line. He'd been out there for about 34 hours. Everyone just went nuts! The Korean guy finally finished and he was bowing and thanking everyone. The rest of the runners were crying their eyes out. All the international flags were flying—seventy nations of people were all dancing to the music and cheering this one guy to finish his race. He was crying and laughing. We all knew the hell he'd been through and it was incredible that he never gave up. It's people like that who are celebrated the most. There's no-one there to greet the first person across the line but the last person will always have a welcoming party. Those are moments you wish you could bottle and show to people. He could easily have chucked it in but he didn't.

After the longest day, we just had a 10-kilometre run around the Pyramids of Giza the next day to finish the race. Megan was totally mangled but she had a grin from ear to ear.

Going around the Pyramids was amazing. It was kind of touristy because we'd driven from the finish line the previous day to run around the Pyramids. The Pyramids were built for the kings and queens of ancient Egypt and it's estimated to have taken 25,000 workers more than 80 years to complete them. After the day before's running, I kind of knew how they must have felt!

It was heavily guarded and we were waiting for ages to run these last few kilometres—I just wanted to get it over with. Of course, I needed to go to the toilet. I'd been standing in line for ages and every time I tried to leave the group, the armed guards quickly had their AK-47s pointed at me. I realised that I was going to have to pee so I went over in this corner by a wall. The guard followed me and I just didn't care. I'd been out running in the desert for so long, I'd lost all my inhibitions. When he realised what I was doing, he turned away and let me get on with it!

After my unscheduled wee stop, we finally got out and ran those last few precious kilometres surrounded by the Pyramids of Giza. Of all the ultras that I've completed, this one was just that little bit sweeter because I completed it with one of my best mates—I always knew Megan could do it and now she knows that, too.

Ultra-race rookie—Megan's story

Given I only started running in February 2009 in preparation for crewing for Lisa at Death Valley, I'm still slightly amazed that I found myself entering the 4 Deserts Sahara Race in 2010. In the past, I had always seen photos and video footage of events like this and thought they were amazing. But I was pretty sure I could never do something like that.

If I hadn't gone to Death Valley with Lisa and coped with that heat and run through there, there was no way I would ever have contemplated doing the Sahara. But having Lisa's support and her belief that I could do this really made a huge difference for me. In fact, it was her idea that I enter the race in the first place. She said to me, 'I'm going to the Sahara, do you want to come?' And I thought, 'Well I've always wanted to go to Egypt so . . . why not?'

The prospect of sharing the race with Lisa as a competitor rather than in a support role was huge for me. Once I'd decided to enter the race, it became an obsession. I spent a heap of time training and the rest of my time I seemed to be thinking about what I'd need to take and how I'd cope with whatever the race threw at me. To make it all work, I split my life into three—there was work, there was training and there was family. And that was really hard. I worked to pay the bills and training can swallow a lot of time but I had to make sure my family didn't miss out.

Before I met Lisa, I never really thought about going overseas. I always felt kind of like I hadn't seen enough of New Zealand. But after going to Death Valley with her, I realised that I really wanted to get out and see the world.

Before the race in the Sahara I spent a couple of weeks travelling around Egypt, acclimatising to the heat and working through the inevitable jet lag. I never really worried too much about travelling there on my own. The resilience of ultra-marathoning and doing jujitsu helped me to cope with pretty much any situation I found myself in so I wasn't as scared as I might have been.

At Sharm el Sheikh, the porter at the hotel said to me, 'Where are your friends, lady?' I told him I didn't have any. And he said, 'No, no, no, sharks in the sea are kinder than the wolves on the street!' Sure enough, I walked out the door and three blokes followed me down the street. I ended up going into another hotel and pretended I was looking for my friend Mary! The trouble was that some of these blokes were in cahoots with the management of some of the hotels so at times it was a bit tricky.

I lost count of how many times I had firearms trained on me while I was travelling. At the time, I didn't realise the issues in Egypt were so bad and I didn't realise that Sinai was one of the chief drug-trafficking parts of the world. I'd go through borders and be tipped out of the vehicle, separated from my guide and they'd take my passport off me. I'd look around and there's all these guys with firearms pointed at me. There was one time, in particular, where these guys put the road spikes out because we were close to a United Nations border security. They were evil. I looked different to the picture on my passport and being a white female travelling on my own they were suspicious of me. They spent thirty minutes standing around me with an AK-47 aimed at me. I realised I couldn't change the situation and I just had to go with the flow. I knew I couldn't move and just had to keep my cool. Eventually they let me go. I've become quite resigned in situations that I can't control.

Getting out into the desert, I pinched myself every day

of the race. I couldn't believe I was there. Day one was really hard. Heaps of elite athletes were pulling out and it made me worry a bit. It was a really hot day and we had a 40-knot headwind that dried everyone out. It felt like being in an oven on turbobake.

At one point, me and this American runner spotted this bush in the distance that looked huge. We quickened our pace towards a bush thinking it would give us some shelter from the sun and the wind. By the time we got to it the bloody thing was only about 50 centimetres high with a patch of shade about 10 centimetres high. We both dived our heads straight into this wee patch of shade and crashed our heads into the bush. Then the pair of us lay there and just laughed and laughed. Then we picked ourselves up, shook off the sand and kept going. It was hilarious that neither of us said a word but knew that we were both thinking the same thing—that kind of silent communication is really common in ultrarunning and it's amazing.

Going into the race, I had several plans. Plan A went out on day one and Plan B went out pretty soon after that. I'd used all my blister kit up on day two, I think. So it was just a matter of keeping going. I had to pace myself and focus on getting to the end of each day.

On day four there was a guy who had crapped out really badly. He was really dehydrated and hyperventilating and determined to carry on no matter what. My paramedic training kicked in so I stopped to help him. The medics at one checkpoint were really worried about him but he was determined to keep going. I told them I was happy to walk with him to the next checkpoint. They said they wanted to keep him there for another half an hour. I said, 'That's fine.' I waited for him and took two extra bottles of water in my pack for him and off we went. The extra weight of the water was a bit more than I would have liked and I did regret it slightly about 2 kilometres into the next stage, but it was worth it to get another runner through to the next checkpoint. Once we got there, I handed him over to the medics and I felt great that I was able to help someone else out even though I was doing it tough.

You do a lot of soul searching in conditions like that. You have to balance out your own needs with the needs of other people out on the course. You do spend a lot of time in your own head and I found my iPod really helps for that. Mind you, listening to Pink Floyd out in the middle of the Sahara— who needs drugs or alcohol? It's kind of surreal.

While I was out there I thought about this old guy I'd met doing an ambulance transfer. He was a returned serviceman and he'd fought in Egypt. It takes one person like that to really get you through your lowest ebb. We had it easy in the Sahara when you think about it. We knew that we were getting water every 10–12 kilometres. We didn't have to worry about getting shot or living in a war zone. That old guy would have been in a far worse situation when he was there, not knowing whether he'd live to make it back to New Zealand. They didn't know where their next water supply was and could only carry what they could carry—all with the added risk of getting shot.

On the longest day, which was a 100-kilometre stage, I'd already fallen over and given myself a huge haematoma on my left thigh. I picked up this little rock that I'd landed on and boy did I curse it! I smashed it until it broke but I didn't feel much better for it. I carried on and there was nobody for two hours in front of me or two hours behind. It's just beautiful knowing that you're so isolated. I felt like I was the only person on the earth. It was totally awesome going through Wadi el-Hitan, the Valley of the Whales. How bizarre—6 million-year-old fossils in an open-air museum. It certainly took my mind off my blistered feet. Pacing myself was the only way I was going to get through as my blisters were too bad. Slowly but surely I made my way onwards through the course, often on my own which was rather cool, actually. It seemed like the best way to absorb the magic of a desert.

But then you've always got that constant sense of danger. Your peripheral vision is massive —it has to be. You're not only looking for the little pink flags, or the glow sticks at night, but you've got to keep an eye on your footing as well. Especially at night, torchlight on white sand means that your depth perception is next to nil and it's very easy to fall over. When I first got my torch out, I found that it had turned itself on and the battery was almost flat. I cursed myself for such stupidity but, thankfully, I had a spare.

Just after I'd fallen over, I noticed what looked like a person just to the right in my peripheral vision. I blinked and thought I had sand in my eye. Everywhere I looked it was still there. I washed my eyes out and had something to eat, checked I wasn't dehydrated or hypoglycaemic and this blimmin' thing was still there. Everywhere I looked I could see it. I could make out the form that was a bit like the Grim Reaper! I felt a bit scared for a while and it worried me that I was seeing this thing and I was out in the desert all alone. Then I thought, 'Oh well, I can't do anything about it, I might as well keep going.' So I just plodded along.

It stayed with me all night. After a while, it actually made me feel like I wasn't alone and I felt quite comfortable in my environment. It never changed—it was the shape of a male with huge broad shoulders. It felt like it was somebody watching over me. When I was with Bedouins in the Sinai, I realised just how spiritual they are as a people. I had visited some tombs with them and I wondered if I'd picked up a good Bedouin spirit along the way—well, that's how I rationalised it in my head. Whatever it was, it stayed there with me the whole way and I felt at peace like I've never felt at peace before.

Early the next morning, I could hear the Egyptian music from a town nearby because I was just near the finish line. As the sun came up over the sand dunes, all of a sudden it wasn't there anymore. It felt quite weird and I actually missed it. I'd never had anything like that happen to me but, since then, I've been much less fearful about things in general. For example, when I get into difficult situations now at work or out on search and rescue jobs, I'm more comfortable and I don't freak out like I used to. From that night, I'm much more fatalistic about things. I feel like if it's going to happen, it's going to happen.

Anyway, I saw this thing go 'poof' in the distance. I thought I was hallucinating but it was a meteor with this huge tail. It went on for quite a while—I'd say five or six seconds. It was really empowering to see it. At the next checkpoint there was a husband and wife having an argument over the meteor. He was telling her she was hallucinating and she was saying, 'I saw it! I saw it!' I told them I'd seen it, too, but I'm pretty sure he thought I was hallucinating as well!

I never thought about crossing the finish line of any of the stages. I thought that would be a bad omen to do that but I did wonder how I would feel.

I had blisters right down to the bone on my big toe so I was just focused on putting one foot in front of the other. I couldn't have gone fast if I'd wanted to. I'd wind myself up into a good pace. Then I'd have to stop at a checkpoint to take on water. Stopping meant that it would take another hour or so before I'd get back into my race rhythm.

If anybody had videoed me they'd have seen a sorry sight. I was stumbling along. At some stages, I was swearing my head off. But then 10 minutes later, my rhythm would be back in and I'd be motoring. At one stage I was doing about 3 kilometres an hour but when I was really into my stride I'd be back up around 6 or 7. Three kilometres an hour was horrible. Think about it—100 kilometres at 3 kilometres an hour . . . not fun.

You can be 5 kilometres from the finish line and not finish a stage. It's never over until it's over. The last 5 kilometres of the Long March were through mud—salt-encrusted mud. It was terrible. I had been feeling elated at being so close to the end and then . . . the mud. Every step was so hard and, to reduce the pain in my feet, I had to keep them as flat as possible. But going through the mud it was impossible to keep them flat—it was absolute agony, but I knew I was really close to finishing so I just kept going.

Lisa was waiting for me at the finish line. As I crawled over the line, I looked up at her and said, 'Lisa, I've never been so fucked in all my life.' I'd done it. My first long day. My time was 26 hours and 22 minutes. I was bloody delighted. From the finish line I managed to get a bit of water down me before crawling over to our tent where I proceeded to pass out for several hours.

After I finally woke up, I went to the foot spa to get my feet patched. The doctor said to me, 'How did you get here?' I thought, 'What a dumb question.' I said, 'I ran . . . well, I walked . . . actually, I shuffled!' He asked me which vehicle I'd come in. I told him I hadn't. He couldn't believe that I'd done the whole last stage with my feet like they were. He reckoned they were the worst he'd seen in a while.

The next day running through the final stage at the pyramids, I thought I'd bawl my eyes out when I finally got to the end. But I was so stuffed that I didn't really think about it. It wasn't until I got back to the hotel that I realised what I'd done. I'd actually finished. Then I cried.

After I came back it took me months to adjust to everyday life. Every day, I still think about the Sahara. I can listen to a certain song and it can take me back to a point in the race. It was just so totally awesome that it's never far from my mind. It's quite hard when you come back—all I wanted to do was see my son. But coming back and realising it's over was hard. Everything that I'd focused on for so long was done.

You've pushed yourself like never before so things can't ever be the same again. I found that for a while I was quite intolerant of people who would give up when things got tough. I started to realise how easy people have life in New Zealand and they just don't see it. I found that frustrating. Working as a paramedic, I would get frustrated by dealing with people who just don't see how lucky they really are. I see too many lives cut short through bad luck, bad management and bad decision-making, so each day I'm reminded of the worth of making each day the best that it can be.

After three days home I was back at the gym, but trying to walk on the treadmill with my manky feet was a bit of a joke! But I just knew that I had to do it. I was back at work straightaway, too. That was good—all my workmates were really proud of me. My parents were stoked, too. You know, you go to a funeral and everybody goes on about how great the person was but, really, why wait until they die to tell them? I got some really touching emails from people in my family and those are things I'll treasure forever. I've saved every single one of them. It was amazing to get those words of encouragement—I'll treasure them always. It made me realise that I need to celebrate each day and all the people in it.

Introduction to electrolytes

Ben Winrow, an Invercargill-based doctor and ultramarathon runner, learned the hard way about the importance of keeping electrolytes balanced while running—you can read his story on page 160. Here, he provides technical information about the most important electrolytes—sodium, potassium, magnesium and calcium—and emphasises why you need to know about them and why you need to keep them balanced while exercising in order to stay alive and maintain good health.

•

Electrolytes and their homeostasis (from the Greek *homeo* or same and *stasis* or stable) is a complex subject that fills whole textbooks—not only biochemical textbooks but also sports science textbooks, and there are countless websites dedicated to electrolyte physiology. These tiny molecules have a major effect on the function of the body in a micro- and macroscopic way. Unfortunately, their consumption and need for replacement is largely situation specific, so running in a desert has a different physiological profile from running, say, in extreme cold.

Just remember that your body is phenomenal and has a myriad mechanisms to protect itself and maintain the status quo, irrespective of the external conditions—be they extreme cold, extreme altitude or extreme heat. Humans are, in every respect, naturally awesome and powerfully driven.

The aim of the following information is not to provide an exhaustive account of the biochemical function of electrolytes, nor is it trying to tell the obsessive how to calculate to the last milligram what they need to replace what they are losing should they be running, for example, at an average pace of 12 kilometres an hour over 80 kilometres with an average wind speed of 25 kilometres an hour and a humidity of 95 per cent at 2000 metres above sea level.

The aim is to inform the new and aspiring runner of the main functions of sodium, potassium, magnesium and calcium so they gain an understanding and appreciation of their significance in any long-distance running ambitions that they, as a runner, may have.

The human body consists of about 40 litres of water and this is known as 'total body water'. In males this makes up about 55–60 per cent of body weight and in females this contributes around 45–50 per cent of body weight. This fluid sits in many areas in the body but, broadly speaking, it is segregated into two major areas: intracellular and extracellular. Basically, this means that there is lots of fluid—around 25–28 litres inside the cells in the body and around 12 litres outside the cells in an average man. How is this maintained? What is the function of all that fluid hiding in different compartments in the body? Why should we care?

Daily intake is very dependent on the individual but, as always, there are averages. Recommended intake is usually around 2.5–3 litres from various sources, including processes that occur inside the cells themselves! This intake is usually balanced by the body's output—in a steady state the body loses fluid in pee and poo, and through breathing and sweating.

The main and most important regulator of the volume and make-up of total body water are the kidneys. As a runner, especially when undertaking very long runs, it is of utmost importance that you look after your kidneys. They have compensatory mechanisms to cope with the electrolyte loss in sweat but, despite thousands of years of perfection of the system and as amazing as their compensatory mechanisms are, you need to understand that they can be overcome under stress. Then, their structure and function can be clogged by the breakdown products of muscle when running.

Be sure you are peeing when you're running, listen to your body and practice, practice, practice with fluid needs and replacement, and nutrition. Be aware that the formulas and calculations don't work. For example, I have ridden a 140-kilometre road cycle race in Belgium on two bottles of fluid and then struggled with the same amount of fluid, in the same weather, with fewer hills on a 60-kilometre ride. I've had similar experiences while running.

Be prepared to change what you think is the right amount to drink or eat depending on how you feel and what is coming out of you. You need to check your wee—if it's dark and concentrated, you need to drink more.

Sodium (Na)

Function

In the body, sodium makes up around 90 per cent of the extracellular solutes. Sodium has many functions in the body but these can generally be summarised by the following three main functions. Sodium:

- helps regulate the pH-acid-base balance
- helps regulate intravascular (inside the blood vessel) volume and, as a consequence, blood pressure
- helps facilitate transmission of electrical nerve impulse.

All three functions are important when we run. Your pH needs to be maintained very tightly or chemical and enzymatic reactions will break down and your kidneys will begin to have trouble. If your pH goes beyond certain limits—and this is usually secondary to disease processes rather than as a result of heavy exercise—there is no coming back.

Sodium is reabsorbed in the kidneys, bringing water with it, maintaining a fairly constant internal environment and helping to maintain blood flow to your organs and your brain.

Sodium, which is a cation—it has a positive electrical charge—helps to maintain an electrical gradient between the inside and outside of a cell so that electrical impulses can be transmitted and muscles, including the heart, can function properly.

Daily requirement

In an average individual the daily sodium requirements are around 90–110 milliequivalents (mEq), assuming that you're not going to be running a long way. This can be gleaned from food, replacement products and can be reabsorbed by or lost from the kidneys to maintain a level of between 135 and 145 mEq/L in your blood.

Does your sodium level change during exercise?

Sweat, gastric secretions if vomiting occurs, and urine are the main ways in which sodium is lost during exercise. So, the more you sweat, vomit and/or urinate, the more sodium you will lose. However, the kidneys regulate urine flow and they can actively reduce the amount they let out.

How much you need is dependent on what you're doing. For example, run in a desert and you sweat more and subsequently lose more sodium. Vomit more, and the same is true. Sweat has a sodium concentration of around 70–80 mEq and vomit around 50 mEq. In terms of what is lost during exercise, sweat is the main contributor to sodium loss and, thus, the main cause of suffering from effects of low sodium if it is not replaced.

How do you know if you have too much sodium (hypernatraemia) or too little sodium (hyponatraemia)?

To define hypernatraemia and hyponatraemia you have to look at fluid status. What this means is that you have to know, or at least suspect, how much total body water, especially intravascular volume, you have because this has a direct effect on the level of sodium in the body.

Hypernatraemia is defined as a sodium blood level over 145 mEq/L. This is usually because you are not drinking enough so you have decreased total body water resulting in a relatively high sodium level, or you are suffering from a fluid deficit because water in excess of your sodium loss is being lost somewhere.

When you are running you need to take on enough water to prevent this—simply put, this means CARRY MORE WATER. You also need to be aware of your sense of thirst, and if you are not as sensitive to thirst as the average bear you will need to make an extra effort to take on fluids.

Symptoms of hypernatraemia include weakness, tiredness, very extreme thirst, and an inability to produce spittle. You may also suffer from a fast heartbeat— tachycardia—and you will probably stop urinating as your kidneys attempt to retain water. Unfortunately, the majority of these symptoms are felt by most competitors in endurance events at some stage.

This is where previous experience and practice come into play. For example, if you have run out of water before or needed to ration your intake, you'll know what thirst is like. Patients with hypernatraemia in a clinical setting, if they are conscious, display thirst much different and more severe than anything you will ever see in an endurance event.

If you have trained well but during the race something

feels different about any of the symptoms described above, then you know you might be experiencing a problem, or are about to. That's why you need to train properly—not just by doing the distance, but by checking your fluid intake and output, trying electrolyte replacement gels, and seeing what other forms of nutrition suit you best. Get these right and you'll be laughing, or at least smiling, at the end of any race.

Hyponatraemia is defined as a sodium blood level less than 135 mEq/L. This is usually more of a medical problem and any rapid correction of the problem may leave you with life-changing consequences, including death, if it doesn't leave you paralysed. Hyponatraemia needs an assessment of the serum osmolarity, and low or hypotonic hyponatraemia is the one that affects runners. The fluid status comes into play and, in terms of running, hypovolaemic—low fluid status— and euvolaemic—normal fluid status—hyponatraemias are important. Hypotonic hypovolaemic hyponatraemia is caused by vomiting, dehydration and sweating. Hypotonic euvolae-mic hyponatraemia is caused by water toxicity. Most of the famous stories of marathon runners falling down into a coma and not waking up are due to this.

Symptoms of hyponatraemia include feeling sick, loss of appetite, painful cramps and a nasty headache. Once again, the first two are common when running anyway. The last two are more noticeable and shouldn't occur on a run or training session, whether it's cross training or race-specific training. If you do begin to experience these symptoms you need to let someone know, and if it worsens you need to stop and seek help.

LOW SODIUM LEVELS CAN KILL—this warning needs to be heeded even though it is rare and only happens in extreme circumstances.

Potassium (K)

Function

Potassium is a key contributor to the resting membrane potential—electrical potential—enabling our cells to transmit the electricity that causes our legs to move, our hands to grip and our hearts to beat. As sodium is the main cation outside cells, so potassium is the main cation inside cells. It is also important in carbohydrate and protein synthesis.

Potassium is regulated by exercise, pH, insulin levels in the blood (which is very important if you're diabetic), plasma osmolality and hypothermia. The latter regulatory mechanisms in metabolism are very important to be aware of as they directly affect us when we run.

Another key point here is that people on certain medications need to be very careful. These medications primarily include, but are not restricted to, diuretics such as furosemide, thiazides and potassium-sparing diuretics. It is of utmost importance to consult your family doctor if you are on any regular medication and you intend to undertake extreme endurance training and exercise.

Daily requirement

The average person needs around 55–95 mEq per day. The most common potassium-rich food is the ever-popular banana. Potassium is mainly excreted, like Na, by the kidneys and you lose around 70 millimoles (mmol) per day. The rate of excretion is helped by secretions from the adrenal glands that sit just above the kidneys. Its levels are very strictly controlled within the body at 3.5 and 5.3 mEq/L. Any deviation above or below this level in a hospital environment is treated as even a small fluctuation can be deadly.

Does your potassium level change during exercise?

Sweating and vomiting cause potassium loss. The levels of potassium can also be changed by the acid balance in your blood, your temperature—especially at altitude or in a cold environment—and the amount of insulin in your blood. All of these parameters change when you exercise.

How do you know if you have too much potassium (hyperkalaemia) or too little potassium (hypokalaemia)?

Hyperkalaemia is defined as a potassium level greater than 5.3 mEq/L. In hospital, if there is a level higher than this you would be given an ECG (electrocardiogram) to see if the hyperkalaemia is affecting the electrical conduction of your heart. Should the level be >6 or if an ECG shows changes you would be treated with medications to push potassium into cells, increase excretion, decrease absorption from the bowel and stabilise cell membranes. Unfortunately, when you are running this isn't really an option and so you have to be guided by other signs and symptoms.

Hyperkalaemia is usually caused by underlying disease processes or concurrent medication use. The main way it affects runners is through excessive intake or replacement. Maybe you are eating too many bananas! Note, you would have to eat a very large amount of them.

Metabolic acidosis—essentially a breakdown of the body's acid–base buffering system—is another cause of hyperkalaemia found in runners after prolonged endurance events. That's why the kidneys must be looked after—if they are damaged while running it may affect their ability to regulate potassium and your pH.

As an aside for diabetics, insulin deficiency is a cause of hyperkalaemia. Please check with your doctor and have a sensible insulin regime if you are going to undertake endurance exercise. It is also important that diabetics don't run alone.

Symptoms of hyperkalaemia are, unfortunately, nondescript, including weakness, tiredness and light-headedness. The higher the potassium level the more apparent the symptoms will become. Should you feel any altered sensation in the extremities, such as numbness or severe weakness, or bradycardia—meaning your heart is beating too slowly for the conditions—you need to stop and seek help or, at least, be very aware of yourself and how you are feeling and be ready to stop if things change. At worst, you could have a heart attack and die.

Hypokalaemia is defined as a potassium level <3.5 mEq/L. The same actions are taken in hospital for hypo- as for hyperkalaemia, but the drugs used to treat it are different.

Again a word of warning for diabetics: if you take too much insulin, not only will you become hypoglycaemic but you'll potentially also run into hypokalaemic trouble. As always, if you are on any medication it is important to discuss your exercise regime with your doctor. As a curiosity, licorice also reduces your potassium, so no licorice treats on long runs.

Symptoms of hypokalaemia include feeling slightly confused and lethargic, tiredness and incredible nausea. You'll notice that with every step your calf muscles begin to hurt much like a pulled muscle, leading to full-on cramping until, eventually, you can't stay on your feet because of secondary muscle weakness. Remember, potassium enables electrical signals to pass down cells enabling muscle function. If the level goes too low you may begin to feel as if your heart is falling down stairs inside your chest, or your heart may miss a beat followed by a strong heartbeat. This is worrying—it shows your heart is having trouble functioning and if potassium levels get lower still, you will die.

HIGH AND LOW POTASSIUM LEVELS CAN KILL and you need to know it! Be aware of yourself and how you feel.

Magnesium (Mg)

Function

Magnesium usually goes hand in hand with potassium. They travel together in the body and inside the cells. Magnesium has numerous important and often-overlooked functions. It helps, along with potassium and sodium, to regulate the level to which sensitive tissues respond to electrical stimuli. It also helps determine the extent to which calcium enters smooth muscle cells, and this is vitally important for muscle function. As more extensive research is carried out, especially in an intensive-care setting, the importance of magnesium is becoming more apparent.

Daily requirement

The average person needs a meagre 20 mEq per day to maintain a level of 1.5–2.5 mEq/L.

Does your magnesium level change during exercise?

Your magnesium level changes with exercise in line with changes to your potassium level. In addition, dehydration leading to low potassium and calcium levels also affects the magnesium level.

How do you know if you have too much magnesium (hypermagnesaemia) or too little magnesium (hypomagnesaemia)?

Hypermagnesaemia is defined as a level >2.5 mEq/L. The main cause of dangerously high magnesium levels is disease, including low thyroid function, renal failure and Addison's disease. However, dehydration, excessive use of certain anti-stomach acid medications and increased intake from replacement products can also put you at risk.

Symptoms may creep up on you. For example, you may be on a run and feel some slight confusion or be sweating a little more than you think you should when you suddenly feel down and out about everything. If something chocolatey or your favourite spread on toast doesn't resolve the situation, then something more serious may be wrong. You may carry on, wondering why you are down and thinking about quitting, when you suddenly realise that gripping your bottle or opening gels or food packs has become difficult. Eventually, if left unchecked, you will fall to the ground unable to move as your breathing muscles cease to function.

This, again, emphasises the need to do long runs and to know your body in an intimate way—not in a sexy-time way, but with an honest knowing of your bodily processes and what you are capable of so that you will be able to recognise when something is seriously wrong.

Hypomagnesaemia is defined as a level <1.5 mEq/L. This is more serious and also more likely to be a problem for runners than hypermagnesaemia. Diarrhoea, leading to concurrent hypokalaemia, is the main cause. Diabetes and drugs also contribute to low magnesium levels. As always, if you are on any medication it is important to discuss your exercise regime with your doctor. The most common symptom of hyper- and hypomagnesaemia is confusion. Low calcium in conjunction with low potassium can cause a seizure, or you may fall into a coma or your heart may stop. If this happens, death will quickly follow.

Calcium (Ca)

Function

Calcium is, by far, the most abundant electrolyte in the body—around 99 per cent of it is found in your bones and teeth. The physiologically active form acts as a messenger for a swathe of physiological and biochemical processes, including helping with coagulation of blood, and the transmission of impulses in muscle tissue including the heart. It is a major player in the contraction of smooth muscle, acting much like a key to open the door of contraction in all your muscles—without calcium, you wouldn't be able to move.

The level of total calcium—made up of 8.4–10.1 mg/dL of bound calcium and 4.4–5.2 mg/dL of the ionised form—is regulated by a wide range of mechanisms, including the parathyroid glands, the kidneys and vitamin D. Without vitamin D, the body cannot absorb calcium.

If you become acidotic, which is easy to do on long runs, the amount of ionised calcium increases and the amount of bound calcium decreases.

Does your calcium level change during exercise?

The body's acid–base balance is regulated, in part, by electrolytes. During exercise it is possible to overcome your body's protective mechanisms and thus derange the regulation of electrolytes, including calcium. This in turn will change its function in the body and could land you in trouble.

How do you know if you have too much calcium (hypercalcaemia) or too little calcium (hypocalcaemia)?

Hypercalcaemia is defined as a calcium level (ionised) >5.2 mg/dL (or 1.3 mmol/L). Medical students learn the rhyme 'Bones, stones, abdominal moans and psychological groans', meaning you get bony deposition, renal stones, abdominal pain that is very non-specific and some people go crazy. The cause that I most often see in my practice is secondary to cancer but there is a range of causes, usually disease related.

Excess vitamin D, for all those supplement addicts out there, chronic renal failure, a long time of doing nothing, and thiazide diuretics all play a part in increasing your calcium levels—these are all chronic processes caused by some underlying abnormality.

Symptoms include light-headedness when standing, feeling confused and drowsy, loss of appetite, extreme thirst, and increased frequency of urinating large amounts. You may become dehydrated and then you may have a seizure.

Hypocalcaemia is defined as a calcium level <4.4 mg/dL (or 1.4 mmol/L). It is more common and has more drastic effects. However, it is relatively difficult to reduce your calcium level to a dangerous level through exercise alone.

The first symptom to look out for is tingling around the mouth. You may also experience flaccidity and weakness, and spasms in the throat before a tetany seizure. If you have any underlying cardiac abnormality, which might increase the risk while running, you need to discuss this with your doctor.

6

A high country hundred

When people ask me why I do it, I tell them that life is a bit of an ultra, isn't it? It's up to you how you choose to run it.

Northburn 100, 26–28/3/2011

Back in 2010, I got an email from a guy in Cromwell who had read *Running Hot* and wanted me to come down and speak to a group of Central Otago locals about my running career. That guy was Glen Christiansen, who manages Cromwell's Golden Gate Lodge. It's fair to say that when I read that email I had no idea it would lead to me becoming one of the organisers of what I think is the toughest ultra-race in the southern hemisphere.

When I went down to Cromwell to speak, I'd been thinking about staging a 100-mile (160-kilometre) race somewhere in New Zealand. At that stage, there was no 100-miler in the country and I thought that New Zealand really needed one if we were ever going to be taken seriously as a nation that produces awesome ultrarunners.

I'd been on the lookout for the right location for my dream race for about a year or so but hadn't managed to find the perfect spot. Of course, I had wanted to hold it in Taranaki but, try as I might, I just couldn't find the right route. The main problem I had in Taranaki was that every potential route I considered would need permission from numerous landowners and I knew that it would just take one person to scupper the whole race.

The first time I met Glen in Cromwell we got on like a house on fire. As well as being a hotelier, he's also a dedicated endurance athlete and he really seemed to understand what drives me as an extreme athlete. And if that doesn't keep him busy enough, he's also the main man driving Tourism Cromwell so he seems to know everyone in the whole district. That came in handy once I started telling him about my plan to stage a 100-miler in New Zealand.

Glen didn't miss a beat, replying, 'We could do it down here.' I looked around me and thought, Holy heck, this is a beautiful place. And the hills surrounding the town would be perfect to provide the massive challenge I was looking for. He was right. We could do it right there.

I'd barely got the words out before Glen was on the phone starting to make it happen. I've since found out that that's fairly typical of people in that part of the South Island. There's no mucking around—if they say they're going to do something, they'll do it, and they'll do it as soon as humanly possible.

One of the first people he called was a guy named Tom Pinckney, who owns Northburn Station, just out of Cromwell. Northburn is a traditional high-country sheep station. While Tom and his wife, Jan, still run 10,000 merino sheep on the station, they have also planted 23 hectares of grapes on the property from which Northburn's renowned wine is produced. And as if that isn't enough, they also have a restaurant and accommodation on site. You'd think with all that going on, they'd have enough to deal with without having a bunch of extreme runners careering across their land for a couple of days a year!

But Glen knew what he was doing when he rang Tom. Despite being a really busy man, Tom is another endurance athlete who has completed the famed Coast to Coast Race. He knows what it takes to train for and complete a really tough race and he understood straightaway what we wanted to do.

Glen, Tom and I got together and talked a bit more about the idea. Their enthusiasm for the project was inspiring and it was obvious that I had the perfect venue and the perfect team to make the race happen. Now I just had to work out the perfect route for the race—something that was really going to challenge every runner that entered the race, and something that would set this race apart from all the other races in the world.

Lucky for me, Tom is a helicopter pilot so he flew me all over the property and we assessed possible routes. It didn't take us long to come up with what I think is the toughest and most spectacular 100-miler in the southern hemisphere. The course is extremely hilly and you go from just above sea level up to about 1600 metres—repeatedly. The one bonus about it being so hilly is that the views from the top are absolutely spectacular. I don't think there's another spot in the country that could provide you with such a variety of terrains in such a beautiful place. It truly is magic.

Just as everything else had fallen into place, we found the ideal race director for what we now called the Northburn 100. Based in Wanaka, Terry Davis has worked in events management for years. Not only that but he had experience in managing 24-hour adventure races and, like the rest of the team, he's also an endurance athlete, having completed the legendary Kepler Challenge among other races. Terry's job was to pull all of the logistics of the race together.

As soon as word got out about what we were doing, the support that we got from the Cromwell community was amazing. The whole township of Cromwell has really got behind it with heaps of locals volunteering to help out on the course and offering whatever help they could. Even if some of them thought we were all absolutely mad, they still made sure all of the competitors were welcome and well looked after.

The first race was held on 26 March 2011. We had 50 runners spread over 50- and 100-kilometre and 100-mile races. The competitors were largely experienced ultrarunners but there were a few marathon runners in the 50- and 100-kilometre races who were keen to step up to the longer distances.

It's a very serious race for a number of reasons. The weather in that area can be extreme, even though it's still early autumn. We had some 100-kilometre an hour winds and sleet coming sideways at the end of the race when we still had five people out on the course. It was really, really cold up the top. Down at the bottom where the winery is it was beautiful and sunny, but up at the top of the course it was blowing a gale and freezing. That's all part of the challenge of a race like this.

Because it was a new event, I don't think some of the runners were prepared for just how hard it was going to be so we had quite a big fallout rate—about 40 per cent. Eventually though, Tracey Woodford from Queenstown won the women's 100-miler with a time of 35 hours 20 minutes 27 seconds and Martin Lukes from Christchurch came in first in the men's 100-miler in 25 hours 44 minutes 35 seconds. They now both have the honour of being the inaugural winners of the Northburn 100.

It has been a really big learning curve for me going from being an athlete to being the organiser of a race. It wasn't dissimilar to the project-management stuff I'd done for the Run Through New Zealand, but there were a lot more factors to consider because I was dealing with 50 runners and not just myself. I've been able to take my experience as a competitor and use it to make the race better. I know what's annoyed me or what's worked for me in the various races I've done and I've taken all that knowledge with me into organising this race. And I've learned an awful lot from Terry Davis about how to run events. He's been my rock when I haven't known where to go or what to do.

One of my main concerns with this race has been safety. I've been in races in the past where I haven't felt particularly safe as an athlete and while what we do is all about taking risks, it's always good to know that if anything goes wrong we'll be looked after. Because of those experiences, I was determined that the preparations for the Northburn 100 be as safety conscious as possible. First, we contracted in an organisation with experience in the field to cover the medical side of it. We had 4-wheel-drive ambulances, helicopters on standby, and we had four doctors on the course as well as plenty of ancillary medics. We were prepared for the dire weather that we ended up having and I was glad that we had taken all the precautions that we had. Even though the race went really well, there's still a few things we learned from it and we'll keep improving.

Running The North Face 100 in Australia really showed me how well a race like this can be managed. There they get 800 runners through mountainous terrain without any major mishaps. I learned a lot watching the guys managing that race and it's great to be able to put some of that knowledge into practice with our 70 runners going through an alpine landscape.

We want to grow this race organically rather than letting it get really huge really fast. Safety is our main priority and we can only ensure that if we have controlled growth year by year of the number of runners taking part. We're also hoping to get more international runners down each year for the race. In 2012, some legends of the ultrarunning community, including Ray Sanchez, Molly Sheridan and Sam Gash, all took part. As our race becomes better known around the world, I feel sure the number of international athletes who take part will continue to grow.

One of the great things with our race is that most people want to come to New Zealand once in their lives and this is a good excuse for runners to come here. It helps that the race is in a really spectacular part of New Zealand and a lot of entrants are adding on little holidays in the area as well. We're doing our best to make sure they're looked after really well while they're here.

Another thing that will help us to attract more international runners is the fact that the Northburn 100 has been appointed as a qualifying race for the Ultra-Trail du Mont-Blanc (UTMB), one of the most famous ultra-races in the world. To gain selection to race in the UTMB, a runner has to get qualification points from completing other races. To qualify for entry, athletes need to have gained six qualification points in the previous year's running. Completing different races around the world will earn a runner different qualifying points—from two to four points, depending on the difficulty of the race. Our race has been given the highest rating of four points. It gives people in Australia and New Zealand a chance to qualify for that big race without having to travel too far. That's great for us. That the Northburn 100 has been judged a four-point race is a real pat on the back for us all and a sign of how well regarded the race is overseas.

Tracey Woodford, winner of the inaugural Northburn 100 women's race

Tracey Woodford, who won the inaugural women's Northburn 100, is someone who knows what it takes to do the hard yards. Like me, she doesn't see herself as a natural athlete and she didn't run her first marathon until 2008, when she was in her early thirties. Back then, she was struggling with her weight and not feeling her best. She decided to make a lifestyle change and take on the challenge of training for a marathon. Before long she realised that with hard work and willpower, nothing was impossible.

After that first marathon, Tracey went on to complete several more marathons. The 60-kilometre Kepler Challenge was her first ultra-race and since then she hasn't looked back. The Northburn 100 was her first 100-mile race and she not only completed it—she won it and came back the following year for more.

When asked about why she does it, Tracey quickly responds, 'You can only know your boundaries by pushing yourself to your limits. This is what I have a passion for and I keep doing it because I can. I love that races allow me to challenge myself and give me an incentive to keep training.'

Here's Tracey's advice on training and nutrition and a few other handy hints for budding runners out there.

Tracey's training tips

I have learned many lessons in the last few years, one of them is to train smart—quality rather than quantity works for me. While some people can run six days a week, I am best running only three to five days a week. I do, however, cross train the other days—a mixture of swimming, aqua jogging, strength training, boxing or biking, snowboarding and skiing in the winter, plus stretching and yoga. I always make sure I include a recovery or rest day once or twice a week. To prevent running becoming a chore and so you don't get bored, make sure you mix it up.

Nutrition

Managing nutrition has, by far, been the most complicated aspect of running for me. I used gels, commercial sports bars and drinks when I first started running. They didn't really work for me as my digestive system doesn't handle them well. Now I make my own gels out of dates, water, chia seeds and lime juice. I also take real food, mostly cooked potatoes loaded with salt, scroggin or nut bars. Nutrition really is a personal choice and it depends at what intensity you are racing at as to what your body can digest. If you are going hard then there will be less blood flow going to the stomach to digest food and if you are going at a lesser intensity you will be able to digest food better. It will take you a while to work out what works best for you so just be aware of the effects different foods have on you as you train and be prepared to tweak your race prep to take that into account.

Handy hints
- Read inspiring articles or books about running—you'll be amazed what you can learn from them.
- Subscribe to running magazines—it will open your eyes to the amazing races out there and present you with new challenges.
- Surround yourself with like-minded people—join a running club or go running with friends.

- Enter shorter races to experiment with food, hydration and how it feels to race with other people.
- An iPod can help with motivation, especially when the legs are feeling tired— just make sure that when you're tired and running on or near roads that you are aware of your surroundings.
- Where the mind goes the energy will flow so think positive and practice positive self-talk, mantras and visualisations.
- Treat your body with TLC—if you expect it to run for miles and miles, treat it well with stretching, yoga, massages and rest.
- Relax and enjoy your exercise and don't take it too seriously—try not to overanalyse what you are doing.
- Be careful with new methods, trends and science reports— 'Keep it simple' is the best motto.
- Fundraise for a cause close to your heart—that will always give you an extra little bit of grit when you think the tank is empty.
- The hardest thing can be just to get out for a run, but once you are out that door it usually doesn't take long to find your mojo—remember you will always feel better after a run.
- Listen to your body—there will be days when you just don't feel like it and it's OK to go home and rest or do something else.
- Train for your race environment—if it's a road run train running on the road, if it's a mountain run train in the mountains; for example, for the Northburn 100 I included big long hill-hiking into my program.
- Remember, you are capable of more than you think you are.
- Last tip, ALWAYS carry loo paper!

Making the transition from marathon to ultramarathon running

I quite often get asked by runners what it takes to transition from marathon running to ultramarathon running. It sounds kind of simple but the longer you're running for, the more pain and exhaustion you have to deal with because the main difference between the two is the amount of time you are on your feet moving.

One important thing I always stress when people ask me about transitioning between the two race lengths is that a good marathon runner won't necessarily be a good ultramarathon runner. But an average marathoner might turn out to be a really strong ultramarathon runner. You will notice that most elite marathon runners are very lithe and small, whereas ultramarathon runners tend to be more muscular and carry a little more substance on their bodies. This is because ultrarunners need their reserves of strength over the longer distances. This is because the longer races require much more stamina, patience and pacing. Some very good marathon runners find it incredibly difficult to go out slowly enough to still be moving at the end of an ultramarathon.

Mental preparation is really important. Sit with the trail maps, think through your strategies, know that there will be pain but also know that there will be a massive feeling of triumph when you cross the finish line. And it is crossing the finish line that should be your only goal in your first ultra.

In terms of prepping for a race, don't do anything more than a 16-kilometre race pace in the eight weeks before a major event. If you want to do a marathon in a build-up, do it only as training. If you've got the discipline to run it that way, fine, but if you're going to race it, don't do it. It's vital that you do it at the pace at which you want to run the ultra. If you're competitive by nature that can be a hard thing to do—it would probably be better to stick to long, slow training runs. Just remember that it's better to go into an ultramarathon slightly undertrained than overtrained as the race will really take it out of you.

About a month out get a blood test done by your doctor. It'll show if you've got any deficiencies. For women, iron is a big one and runner's anaemia can be a problem. When you're running, you're smashing the blood cells in your feet and it can cause anaemia. When you lack iron, it affects the oxygen-carrying capacity of your blood because your red blood cells aren't up to the task. This can affect your performance quite drastically. It can make you lethargic and make you not want to train.

In the last three weeks before an event, you need to taper well—you're not going to be getting any fitter in that time but you can overtrain and cause injury. Do lots of rehab stuff in that time. Get any niggles sorted out before you race. Sleep and sleep and sleep. Take your supplements. For your joints, I recommend glucosamine and chondroitin, and flaxseed or salmon oil. Make sure your electrolytes are on track.

Don't worry about racing or what time you'll do. They both require a lot of strategy and experience and are easy to get wrong. Just focus on going the distance and finishing the race. Going out slowly and tapering off is the key as when you're standing at the start line bouncing with adrenaline and energy, it's impossible to imagine just how fatigued you will feel late in the race. Energy conservation is what is needed to finish an ultra.

No matter how long an ultra is, the last 20 kilometres are the key to success. It doesn't matter how fast you go for the rest of the race if you have got nothing left in the tank for the last 20. I always try to break the effort required for a race down into percentages. For example, in a 100-kilometre race, I'll try to expend 20 per cent of my energy in the first 50 kilometres, 30 per cent in the next 30 kilometres and have 50 per cent of my energy left for the final 20 kilometres. This might sound a bit strange but in my experience the last 20 kilometres are almost always harder than the first 20.

Plan to run the last 20 kilometres without your speed falling drastically, but know that those last 20 will probably take more mental strength and determination than any marathon you have experienced.

Electrolytes, nutrition and training— personal experience from a doctor's perspective

Dr Ben Winrow competed in the 2012 Northburn 100. While he was there, we got chatting about some of the medical aspects of ultrarunning, in particular, nutrition and hydration. (He contributed the information about electrolytes on pages 136–148.) Here's his personal account of how he learned the hard way to balance his fluid and nutrition requirements to get through serious training and competing in extreme events without hitting the wall.

Ben's story

Everyone is different. Every runner has different preferences, different strengths, different weaknesses and different coping mechanisms to maximise their strengths and improve on their weaknesses. The following is an account of two moments in my own life—one painful and one unexpectedly joyous—that show how far practice and training can take you.

I began running two years ago, mainly to strengthen my legs for cycling. I raced in a duathlon, which was an 8-mile run, a 24-mile ride and a final 8-mile run. With minimal running training it hurt, it really hurt, but I finished. This led me to wonder how far I could push this running business. 'How hard can it be?', I thought.

I was always fascinated by the diametrically opposed schools of thought, one suggesting rigorous training and years of running before attempting anything long distance, and the other suggesting mental strength triumphs over physical difficulty over the long haul. Prompted by a friend who said I would never be able to run long distances due to my body shape—short and stocky—and inspired by the latter school of thought, I entered my first ultra. I had two months from the duathlon to train for a 64-kilometre jaunt through the Brecon Beacons in Wales.

I didn't keep a training log, but from memory I ran maybe three long runs, the longest being 35 kilometres over the hills—this killed me. I ran maybe twice a week, and I had no idea how to taper so didn't do any exercise in the two weeks prior to the run. I had no idea about carrying fluid, I had no idea about nutrition or electrolyte replacement. I was firmly entrenched in the 'if I want it enough I can do anything' camp.

Race day came and I started well. I followed some experienced looking gents who seemed to be walking up the hills—which was new to me—and kept with the action in the second main pack. At about 25 kilometres in I began to falter. My stomach started churning. Was I hungry? Was I feeling sick? I didn't know and I couldn't work it out as I hadn't been here before.

I forced down an energy gel—I was using cycling nutrition for the run—and suddenly at 32 kilometres both my calves started cramping. I had to run with almost motionless legs for fear of sparking off shooting, tearing, agonising arrows of pain into my tired legs.

Thankfully, I had brought some sports beans—high carb and electrolyte jelly beans—and not knowing what was in them, I necked them. I also didn't know that you needed to consume water with them. My cramps were cured by the electrolytes in the beans but I found myself facing a new enemy, abdominal pain, and the want to vomit due to having ingested too much sugar.

I reached the 42.2-kilometre mark and was feeling haggard. Feelings of sickness were replaced by the acute onset of pain in my left knee and right anterior tibial tendinitis, which prevented me from doing anything other than walking on the downs. I wanted to finish— mentally I was there but physically I was failing.

The weather turned on the final ascent. Complete whiteout at the top and a period of getting lost did not help my morale or my condition. But I kept on, staying on the heels of a fantastic running companion who was also doing her first ultra—we kept each other company until the 60-kilometre mark when she went on ahead.

The last 4 kilometres were the biggest mental challenge I have ever faced. I embraced it. I remember hobbling down an old country road full of cobbles, ankles all over the place, the pain unbearable. I sat down and wept with joy, pain, misery and relief. I knew I was only around 2 kilometres from the finish now. I sidled along a river, knowing it was the home stretch, limp-running before turning a corner and seeing the finish line. I came forty-third out of about 80, I think. I felt such relief, but had been so close to failure. I was injured for three months and have never truly got a normal left knee back.

From this experience I learned two things:

You can do it.

You need to practice, not just running but including nutrition, electrolytes, gear, and mixed physical training.

First of all, to anyone out there wanting to do something—YOU CAN DO IT. If you want it enough, you can make it happen. Having said that, nutrition, endurance, electrolytes, clothing, gear and distance all require practice. In combination, your drive and determination and the foundation you lay, with practice, will lead to success.

My last ultra—the 2012 Northburn 100—was a different story. I by no means consider myself an outstanding athlete. I feel quite mediocre and am happy with my lot. The only thing I ask of myself is to find where my limits are, to live and train and race in them and to feel like I'm living, rather than just existing.

I signed up to the Northburn 100-kilometre distance in a fit of 'I have done nothing with my year so far'. I also signed up to 120-kilometre and 140-kilometre road-bike races, two mountain marathons and a practice 50-kilometre loop of the 100-kilometre Northburn course, along with various local bike races, some 10-kilometre running races and two half marathons. I had never run anything other than the duathlon and the Welsh ultra. I had four months to train, with the aforementioned races acting as training runs rather than races.

And so I began to run . . .

The first 10-kilometre run I did was alone, dark, early in the morning and wet. My immediate thoughts were, 'What the hell am I doing? I am not fit enough and I can't even run 10 kilometres without being in pain and short of breath.'

I found a running buddy and we sourced some interesting local runs with small hills and flats, and we attacked these with regularity. Meanwhile, I read books and did some internet research. I found the literature and the internet very confusing and so decided to write my own schedule, with only three requirements. I need to be able to:

- eat while I run
- replace my electrolytes
- keep my expectations and training jumps low.

I began to look at what was in energy bars—what food might give me the most energy? And what would be the lightest to carry? I thought about clothing and minimum gear for the first time. On every run, no matter how short, I filled a bladder to the brim, put in the minimum gear required for the Northburn and played around with the position of various elements of my gear. I began to plan my weekends around being able to run up a mountain or do a long run along a flat path while my friends were out 'enjoying' themselves.

I'm not going to lie: there were times when I was tired, there were times when I worked a fifteen-hour day and didn't do anything for the next two, there were night shifts and, on more than one occasion, I fell out of love with the whole thing. I remember after writing my own training log, two weeks went by where I hardly ran at all and just cycled—I didn't want to run. In hindsight I think I was overtraining. I began to get down if I hadn't met the weekly average I'd set myself, and many times I had to take a step back and tell myself that this was for fun as I had promised never to take myself too seriously.

So when the day of the Northburn 100 came, in training I had run over 1300 kilometres, cycled around 2000 kilometres and swum around 30 kilometres—swimming is insanely good for the heart.

I was aching on race day. It was 4 a.m. when I got up,

bleary eyed and nervous. I forced down a bowl of my favourite muesli and a banana. I had my kit list in front of me and my nutrition plan worked out from practice on my long runs (which, as it happens, went completely out of the window on race day). I also had a note from my greatest supporter stating, 'Come on, Ben, run faster, ya pussy!'—great motivation!

I was sick with nerves as I put on my pack with five minutes to the off, feeling its weight and looking around. I felt that I didn't qualify to be here—the crowd looked keen and professional. I was intimidated.

The race started with a 5-kilometre loop back through the start/finish line. I felt good, my legs felt good. I felt like I could run all day—needless to say I would be, and into the night, too.

Someone once told me, 'Don't think about the distance, just enjoy the journey,' and enjoy it I did. The rain was intermittent, the views were spectacular, the 100-kilometre per hour winds on top were insane and took my breath away, the people along the way were interesting and wonderful; a certain camaraderie exists in precious moments during these experiences that I have found nowhere else. You also see things that last only a moment but replay in your mind over and over. One such moment for me on the Northburn 100 was seeing a double rainbow, where the bottom rainbow was flat along the ground and the second just flirted with the sky. I thought, 'Where else would I rather be than here?' I ran out of fluid 2 kilometres before the end of the first loop and so swaggered in feeling strong, but hot and thirsty.

A pit stop with some encouraging words, a protein shake, a banana, some more anti-chafe cream and refills all round and I was off.

I had managed to have one salt tablet in 500 millilitres of

water every 25 kilometres to replace sodium, potassium, magnesium and calcium and I kept down some food, although nausea is always a problem for me from 21 to 50 kilometres.

There were moments on the second 50 kilometres that I wanted to stop and be transported back to the start. Every checkpoint reached was a blessing and not enough can be said for all the volunteers at ultra-distance events. Maybe they don't know what they can bring to the weary racer but many times I was thankful for a simple kind 'Hello' and the concerned 'Are you OK?'.

At 70-ish kilometres I asked how many people were in front of me, wondering how I was going; I genuinely had no idea and was coming up out of a section aptly and accurately called 'the loop of despair'. I was told there were only nine in front of me. I was astounded, I was energised, but I was sure they were wrong. But hey, I was here for fun.

It got dark as I reached the top again—where I wanted to be at this time. It was cold, really cold. I had numb feet and my hands were freezing. I knew there were 16 kilometres to go and this gave me strength. Along the top the wind was so strong I took nearly an hour to run/walk 3 kilometres.

As I began my descent, I opened my bottle of flat Coke—it's my ultimate mood lifter, but it's important I don't drink it too early—and ran. I ran for all I had. I was determined to leave myself on the course. It was the longest and most painful 13-kilometre descent I have ever done. I had to stop several times to bend over, letting out a cry as the pain in my quads got too much. I saw some glow sticks in the distance and I knew the end was nigh. I rounded a corner after a short up and saw the tent, heard the chatter and knew I had made it. I, an averagely fit, mediocre man, had made it. I came in to greet my friends who had kindly waited up for me and we celebrated.

I then approached the organisers to find out where I had come.

Second—17 hours 17 minutes and some odd seconds and I had come second. Never in my wildest dreams did I think that was possible and yet it was real. I put this down to three things:

- Practice.
- Practice.
- More practice.

I remain injury free. I listen to my body: if it aches, I take the day off—rest is as important as a long run. I use compression tights post-run and also endure contrast showers—super cold on my legs, much like Lisa's ice baths—as I find it reduces my recovery time.

Asked if I would do it again, I said: 'No, I'm going to sign up to the 100-miler next year!'

And you can do it, too.

7

Running in the Blue Mountains

If you want to give it a go—do. Take that first step and keep taking those steps. And don't give up the first time you fail.

The North Face 100, 14–15/5/2011

The next big race on my schedule was The North Face 100 in Australia's Blue Mountains. For a desert runner like me, a race like this was always going to be tough. And it was only because of my mate Dean Karnazes that I was there.

I met Dean for the first time when I was running the Badwater Ultramarathon. I was a Death Valley rookie and here was the guy who was the sport's biggest star. I was starstruck to meet him. Fast-forward a wee while and I found myself interviewing him for New Zealand television. We hit it off really well and, since then, he's been incredibly supportive of my running career. One of the things I love about our sport is that everyone does what they can to help each other out.

Dean and I have kept in touch since meeting again in New Zealand. He knew that I was planning some really big races and he also understands how hard it is to get sponsors on board to support big missions. The North Face are huge supporters of his and he clearly saw the potential in me to be a great brand ambassador for them. Good old Dean put in a good word for me with The North Face team in Australia and I am now one of their sponsored athletes. They're the most prestigious outdoor brand in the world so it was a huge honour for me to be part of their team.

I always knew that ultrarunning was big in Australia but until I went to The North Face 100, I had no idea just how big. The race is huge. Every year, more than 800 entries sell out within weeks of opening and there's a huge waiting list for people to get a spot. Lucky for me, The North Face kept one of those spots for me. It proved to be a really good build-up race for my next planned race in the Himalayas because it was ten weeks out from my leaving to go to India.

Mum came over with me, and my cousins from Sydney, who are like sisters to me, were there, too. Mum, Kim, Victoria and their families were my support crew for the day which was absolutely fantastic.

The race starts and finishes in the township of Leura, just out of Sydney. It then winds its way up and down the hills and canyons of the Blue Mountains before ending up back in Leura. Over the 100 kilometres of the race, the trail climbs and descends more than 4500 metres.

Starting at 7 a.m., I was shocked at just how cold it was. I thought heading to Australia it would be nice and warm—boy was I wrong! I guess that it was being held in the mountains should have been a clue but I learned my lesson on that one.

The Spanish ultrarunner Kilian Jornet was there. He's just 24 years old and is like the rock star of the mountain-running world. He's won the Ultra-Trail du Mont-Blanc for the last four years and is an incredible athlete. Just to see someone like that race is amazing. Kilian went on to win the race with an incredible time of 9 hours 19 minutes and 6 seconds. I couldn't even comprehend running that fast. Guys like Kilian are the new generation of superstars and they're pushing the boundaries way beyond anything that's been done before.

It was a really hard event for me because it's single trail and mountainous. The Blue Mountains are absolutely spectacular and running up and down the canyons is stunning, but I'm much better suited to longer races on the road or across deserts. Mountain running and I don't get along at all, and 100 kilometres is a bit too short race for me—I'm slow over that distance. All that climbing and descending is really hard on my asthmatic lungs. I find straight consistent climbing OK because my lungs adjust to it, but going up and down repeatedly is really difficult because my lung capacity doesn't allow me to change gears rapidly enough.

One of the things I love about this kind of event is the conversations I have with other runners out on the course. I was amazed how many of them had read my first book, which was really cool.

It was a fabulous and spectacular race but it was gruelling and quite technical for me. When I'm running in the desert, I can pretty much run wherever I like so long as I'm going in the right direction. In a race like this, which is along a single narrow trail, I have to concentrate a lot more. I have to keep an eye out for tree roots and rocks along the path and because

I'm not that coordinated, I find it quite hard to get up any real speed on the downhill sections of the race.

The worst thing that happened to me was that my light gave out in the middle of the night, so I had to run through this mountainous landscape in pitch dark. I was terrified and all I could think was that it would be a miracle if I got through it without injuring myself, but I did. It turned out to be a great build-up race for the Himalayas. I was stoked to finally finish in 18 hours and 23 minutes. That's not a great time for me but it was a buzz just to finish this race. Despite hitting the finish line in Leura at 1.23 a.m., my support crew were there to cheer me home. They really were amazing. The freezing temperatures were OK for me because I had all the North Face gear with me so I was warm, but my support crew were out in the freezing cold for the whole day and half the night.

My lasting impression of running The North Face 100 is just how incredibly well run it is. The logistics of getting 800 people through that mountainous terrain on a single trail without any major catastrophe is quite a feat.

The next day I was scheduled to do a photo shoot for The North Face with Australia's best outdoor photographer, Mark Watson. I was excited to do the shoot but I was knackered from running. The shoot started at 5 a.m. and, even though I was stiff and sore, Mark got some amazing shots.

Mark didn't get his reputation as an amazing photographer for nothing. It was an epic shoot and we were still out in the mountains at eight o'clock that night. He wanted to do some long exposure night shots of me running in the evening light. While Mark was taking what he thought was going to be the second-to-last shot of the night, the combination of my tiredness from racing and being blinded by the camera flash made me jump in the air and I came down on a rock, rolling my ankle badly in the process. I just remember hearing a loud crack and falling down in a screaming heap. When I hit the ground, I was in a world of pain and all I could think was that I had to leave for India in ten weeks' time. After making it through The North Face 100 in one piece, it seemed completely ridiculous that I'd injured myself doing something as straightforward as a photo shoot.

The immediate problem for me though was that we were about 3 kilometres higher up a mountain than our parked car. Mark had all his camera gear to carry down, and there was no way that I could walk 3 metres let alone 3 kilometres. There was only one thing for it—Stephen Winnacott, the sponsor manager from The North Face, who was with us on the shoot, had to carry me all the way down to the car. Given that he's not that much bigger than me, he really went beyond the call of duty for one of his athletes that night. I won't ever be able to thank him enough for the way he helped me that night.

Once we were off the mountain it was straight to hospital for me. I was in so much pain that I really thought I'd broken my ankle. The team at the accident and emergency unit in Katoomba x-rayed my ankle and it turned out that it wasn't broken after all. I was relieved at that, but then they told me that I'd torn the ligaments on both sides of the ankle. I was gutted. Ligaments take as long to mend as bones and I had just over two months before I was due to fly to India.

Preventing injury

There's so much around what we do that can help us improve our running. The older I get the less resilient I am so I have to spend more time doing rehab on my body. Spending time training and racing aren't enough to keep me race fit anymore. It's really important for me to take time out from that and work on my body. I have to be more careful to take the time to let my body recover after races and I have to be aware of the messages that my body is sending me. Even though I hate taking time out from running, and I'm in my sport because I love doing it, I know that I sometimes have to not run. It's hard to admit that I don't bounce back as fast as I used to, so making the time for massages, sitting in the sauna, stretching, acupuncture, physio and chiropractors is important. Pretty much whatever it takes to help my body I'll do so that I can keep running. The time spent on keeping my body working properly is as important now as putting in the miles. I try to schedule that time as tightly as I schedule my running. It's become just another form of training for me.

One thing I really recommend is that everyone should go to a knowledgeable trainer or Pilates instructor and get a postural assessment done. This assessment will help you to work out whether you have any muscle imbalances in your body. It will show you where you favour certain muscles, thereby making other muscles lazy. Runners often have lazy glutes and strong quad muscles. Another problem area for runners is in the hamstrings—again caused by having strong quads. Once you've worked out these imbalances, a good trainer or instructor will be able to give you exercises to help you get your body back in balance. This will help to prevent injury.

How Lisa copes with asthma

There are thousands of asthmatics out there who have been told that running can trigger asthma attacks and they shouldn't run because of it. But having asthma does NOT mean you can't run. Of course, there are certain precautions you should take when taking up running, but don't let your asthma stop you from trying. There are many shining examples of runners who have achieved incredible results despite their asthma. Two who spring to mind are world record ultramarathon runner Sharon Gayter and world record marathon runner Paula Radcliffe.

I have battled with asthma since I was about two years old. It was so severe when I was a child that I was in and out of hospital all the time. I think that being so ill as a child has had a strong influence on my personality because I had to fight to live the sort of life that others took for granted. I had to learn to control it as best I could and to remain calm in often dire situations—that's been a good start for me to develop my life as an ultrarunner.

If you suspect you are an asthmatic but haven't been diagnosed, make sure you see a doctor because other problems can also mimic the symptoms of asthma.

But if you have been diagnosed with asthma, the following guidelines on medication, warming up and prevention should help you with your running.

Medication

Asthma medication relaxes the muscles around your airways. Asthma causes these muscles to constrict and asthmatics feel like they can't breathe in or get air out. If you aren't an asthmatic, try going for a run while breathing through a straw and you will know what I mean.

There are two types of medication. If you have chronic asthma, you may need a daily preventative medication, like an inhaled steroid; these have side effects so make sure you are fully informed about any medication you are given. The other type is a quick relief asthma medication which acts rapidly to relieve symptoms. These can also be used a as a prophylactic before going for run to help you run without developing asthmatic spasms.

Just make sure that you always follow medical advice given to you when your inhaler is prescribed. Always have your inhalers with you and, if you are prone to really severe attacks, try to carry a cell phone or run with a friend. If you do have a severe attack, stay as calm as you can. Panic can really exacerbate the symptoms. If you are new to this problem, you should know that slowing your breathing and concentrating on breathing out helps. If you need to, sit down but stay upright. Whatever you do, don't lie down—lying down can make it harder for your lungs to work.

Warming up

Asthmatics need to warm up for longer and slightly more intensely than non-asthmatics in order to deal with the sudden race pace from the start. Getting your lungs working hard before your race or intense training can help. It may cause a mild attack, but once you calm down again it's unlikely you will have another reaction that severe during the race. I find this can control my asthma for 4–6 hours.

Prevention

Asthmatics are often allergic to pollen so try to avoid racing when pollen counts are high. During the high pollen-count season, try running early in the morning when there's less pollen in the air. Taking antihistamines can also help but beware of taking any medication for prolonged periods.

I also run with a buff over my mouth, which takes a bit of getting used to and can make you look like a bandit, but it really helps as it stops the pollen entering your airways. As an added bonus it protects your skin from the sun so you don't get burnt. A covering over the mouth also helps keep the moisture in your mouth and prevent dehydration.

Buffs or a mouth covering can also be useful when running in cold temperatures—cold air entering the lungs can really trigger asthma attacks. That's one reason I have predominantly gone for races in a hot, dry climate, like deserts. Out there, there's very little pollen and the air has a very low moisture content.

Preparing for race day

Runners quite often ask me what's the best way to prepare for race day. Everyone has their own processes they go through and for me, as an ultrarunner, it can be quite a complex exercise, so I've asked my good friend Rajat Chauhan, founder of La Ultra The High, the ultramarathon in the Himalayas, to outline his process for raceday preparation.

His three basic rules are:
- Don't try anything new on race day—stick to the methods that worked for you during training.
- Get familiar with the route on the map and how you will get to the starting point.
- The day before the race, take it easy—if you've been training, you've done enough but, if you really must, limit yourself to a 1–2 kilometre run in the morning and don't train in the evening.

7.30 p.m. the night before

Pack your bags—you'll need three small bags to fit into one lightweight and waterproof bag. One bag is for the stuff you'll need in the morning, one is for the things you will need during the race and the third is for the stuff you'll need after you cross the finish line.

Do not pack anything new, especially T-shirts or shoes, for the day of the race—everything you pack should have been tried and tested during your training runs, and not just once but several times. Here's a list of items you are likely to need in each bag:

Morning/pre-race bag

Full-sleeve T-shirt or tracksuit top

Track pants

Mobile phone

Water bottle

Large bin liner—if it's cold, a bin liner works very well to keep you warm while you wait for the run to begin and you won't mind discarding it as you set off

For men—thick cream, such as Nivea, or petroleum jelly, such as Vaseline, or micropore tape to protect your nipples as bleeding from friction is not unusual, and is not just embarrassing but painful, too

Running bag

Running shoes

Socks

Dry-weave T-shirt—not cotton

Bib with your participant number attached by four safety pins to the corners—on the back of your number write your name and the phone number of a person to contact in an emergency

Shorts

Sunglasses—it'll get quite bright after 7 a.m. or so, but only bring sunglasses if you're used to wearing them while you run

Cap—if you are used to wearing one while you run

Belt pouch with on-the-run snacks inside

After-race bag

Water bottle

Dry snack foods, fruit, cereal bars, etc.

A complete change of clothes, including a fresh set of underclothes and a pair of comfortable slippers or floaters

Set of adhesive bandages for blisters and minor cuts

8 p.m. the night before

Eat a carbohydrate-rich dinner—the 'traditional' marathoners' choice would be pasta or pizza, but rice is great as well.

8.30 p.m. the night before

Call the people you intend to carpool with and confirm arrangements—who? where? when? Also ask a friend or a co-runner or participant to call you at 5 a.m., as a back-up plan in case your alarm clock experiences sudden death or you roll over and hit the snooze button.

9 p.m. the night before

Set an alarm for 5 a.m. and go to bed early.

5 a.m. on race day

Rise and shine and take your own sweet time in the loo.

Also take stock—are you feeling good? Most medical emergencies during races occur because people were unwell

but did not wish to miss the event. If you tick any of the following, please don't run:

- Feeling feverish
- Having flu-like symptoms
- Feeling nauseous
- Having diarrhoea
- Feeling chest pain

Even if you are raising money for charity, or running to prove
a point to yourself or to your friends, it is unfair to your
sponsoring charity and the race support staff if you become a
medical emergency on the track. There are many other races
that you will be able to compete in.

5.30 a.m. on race day

Do a final pack and check—double-check your packing list
and the contents of your bags.

Pack your belt pouch with your choice of mid-marathon
nutrition. Typically, that might include:

- 1 sports drink
- 2 cereal bars
- 1 handful of non-sticky, semi-soft candy, such as jelly
  beans, wine gums or jelly babies
- 1 simple sandwich, such as jam, butter or cheese
- A couple of pieces of fruit, such as bananas (a runners'
  favourite), apples or oranges
- 2 handfuls of dried fruit

5.40 a.m. on race day

Eat your breakfast . . . or not—this is a personal choice.
Some people like to eat a bit before the run, others don't. It is

actually important to practise your pre-race snack, too, during training, to find out what works best for you.

If you do eat breakfast or would like to bring something along to eat in the car, it is advisable to choose a light snack. Ideally you want about 250–300 grams of carbohydrates, but very little fibre to avoid causing a stomach upset. No need to fix anything special—just have something high-carb for energising, similar to the items you'd carry on your run, or maybe a low-fat fruit yoghurt.

Some people would like to eat but find it difficult because of nerves. In this case, try a liquid meal such as a fruit smoothie or fruit and yoghurt drink.

6 a.m. on race day

Leave home—make sure you get to the venue in good time, taking into account various road blockages due to the race route, and then give yourself time to find a car park . . . you don't want to be racing to the start line.

6.30–7 a.m. on race day

Check in your bags and get to the start point early—these races do start on time.

On your mark . . . and drink up—use your waiting time to stay well hydrated. Drink 250 millilitres of water or a sports drink in sips over the next half-hour—but don't gulp your drink down right before the race.

7.30 a.m. and the rest of the race

Start running . . .

Start slower than what you know you are capable of— you'll have enough distance and time to catch up.

First aid will probably not be needed if you have followed

a training program faithfully, but if you do find you need medical attention go to one of the race's first aid posts, located at various points along the route.

Drink some water. There are usually water stations positioned every 2 kilometres. Take a few sips at every station, but don't drink all that's in the cups or you'll overdo it. Even in half marathons, overhydration can be a very big problem amongst novice runners. Having too much water to balance the sodium salts in your body can cause a rare but fatal condition called hyponatraemic encephalopathy, and this leads to water retention in the brain. Just be guided by your thirst, not your apprehension.

The stations are long, so don't stop at the start, where it's crowded. Go on ahead and you will find a spot that is free. When you are going to stop, look behind and move to the side, out of the way of other runners so they needn't collide or swerve to avoid you.

Don't take more than one drink if you can help it. Consider the others behind you—you can always get a refill at the next station.

Don't glug it all down—take the drink with you to sip as and when you need to.

When you discard your drink, do so carefully. It's easy for runners to trip over a cup or bottle in their path or bump into another runner who suddenly swerves into their path to avoid discarded drinks.

Say thanks to the people manning the stations—they are all volunteers and are out there to make it an enjoyable day for you.

Eat: if you take any longer than two hours for 21 kilometres, please eat! Forgoing food is not heroic, merely dangerous to you and potentially a nuisance for others who may have to tend to you when you faint. Sports drinks, cereal bars, jam sandwiches, pieces of fruit, handfuls of dried fruits—remember the belt pouch? Have your first snack around 30 minutes into the race and aim for 30–60 grams of carbohydrate per hour to be consumed at regular intervals throughout the race.

At the finish line

Finish . . . and keep walking. Don't just stop short as soon as you cross the line. You need to cool down, and this way other runners coming in are less likely to barrel into you, too.

Change into warm, dry clothes. Get to the baggage area as soon as you can—where you should get your kit—and then head for the reunion area.

Celebrate what you've achieved. However, while spirits are high, it is easy to forget about recovery. Don't.

Recovery

Drink water or fruit juice in moderation, NOT large amounts. You should rehydrate gradually over the 24–48 hours following the race. Eat salty food and space out your drinks to regulate your isotonic balance. If juices taste too acidic, dilute them with water. But remember—water will replace fluids as well as any commercial drink.

Eat within four hours, ideally sooner. It's most important to have proteins within the first hour to help your muscles recover. After that, you need carbohydrates to top up your depleted glycogen reserves.

Recover . . . over the next two days. Yes, it takes that long for your muscles to recuperate, with lots of carbohydrate-rich foods and rest. Of course, this means you have plenty of time to relax, and you don't need to run to recover.

8

Getting High in the Himalayas

It's not about competing against each other and it's cer-
tainly not about money, because there is none. It's a lust
for adventure and wanting to know your limits. It's about
pushing your boundaries.

La Ultra The High, 11–13/8/2011

Following my injury in the Blue Mountains, my recovery was a real race against time if I was going to compete in the world's highest-altitude ultramarathon in the Himalayas. It was just ten weeks until I was due to take on what would possibly be the biggest challenge I'd ever fronted up to.

La Ultra The High is a 222-kilometre race over one of the world's highest mountain passes in Kashmir, northern India. It had been run just once before with only three runners, and only one of the runners managed to finish the race. I knew that the previous year the altitude had knocked the hell out of everyone. I had also heard that when Rajat, the race director, first started to plan the race, he asked the Indian army, who are based and train up there, what their thoughts were. He was told in no uncertain terms that it was humanly impossible to run that distance at those altitudes non-stop—runners would need time to adjust to the altitude at stations along the way.

As a desert runner with asthma, running at 5400 metres, where oxygen levels are roughly 60 per cent of what they are at sea level, this was going to be entirely new territory for me. And if there's one thing I love, it's a huge challenge—this was certainly going to be a new one.

Adding to the altitude, the race promised extremes in temperature. The trail crossed high-altitude desert, which could be as warm as 40° Celsius, but then up on the pass the temperatures could drop as low as -10°.

Aside from the challenge of it all, the fact that the race was in the Himalayas was a massive drawcard for me. I had dreamed of visiting the high mountains since I was a teenager so, once again, I can thank my running for making some of my dreams come true.

Mark Cockbain, who I'd run with in Death Valley and Niger, had been the only runner to complete the 2010 La Ultra the previous year. When I heard about the race, I wrote to Mark straightaway and he strongly recommended that I have a go at it. He told me it was the most incredible experience of his life and that he'd found it really hard. I knew that if Mark said it was hard, it must have been bloody hard. He confirmed what I already knew—I had to give it a go.

The race is invitation only, and to qualify for it you have to have completed one or more of the following races: Badwater Ultra, Leadville 100, Marathon Des Sables, Western States, Spartathlon, the Yukon Arctic Ultra, the Ultra-Trail du

Mont-Blanc (UTMB) or the Annapurna 100. I'd done Badwater twice and completed the Marathon des Sables so I knew that I had what it took.

But before I could even think about what it would be like to race in the world's highest mountains, I had a hell of a lot of rehabbing to do. Before I stuffed my ankle I was running between 110 and 170 kilometres a week. My training is usually based around two long, slow back-to-back runs on the weekends, often on mountains with heaps of trail and ascent, then two interval training sessions during the week interspersed with another one or two 15–20-kilometre runs of intermediate intensity.

After I got home from Sydney, I was on crutches for a few days and then I spent two weeks where all I could do was limp—no long training runs for me at that stage, that's for sure. I started cycling on the exercycle and doing aqua jogging quite soon to try to strengthen that ankle.

I then went and had rehab sessions with Josh Paurini, who ended up joining my crew for the Himalayas. Josh is a personal trainer and he'd had a similar injury so he knew exactly what I could do with it. No-one was very positive that I was going to make it to the Himalayas except me. I knew La Ultra was going to involve a lot of walking rather than running, so I had faith that I could strap my leg up and get over the line somehow—with walking sticks, if need be!

In order to acclimatise myself to the extreme altitude, thanks go to Jeff at Butch Pet Foods who kindly sponsored a Hypoxico Altitude Training System tent for me. These tents simulate the oxygen-reduced air at altitude. You can sleep in the tent and there's also a mask you can wear while training. At the beginning I made a big mistake. You're meant to go gradually and allow the body to gradually adjust to lower and lower oxygen levels as it simulates altitude levels, but I didn't seem to be reacting to it. Also, I thought that perhaps because I'd suffered from asthma all my life, I was used to struggling for air. I talked to my ex-husband, Gerhard, who had trained in a tent like this before. He told me to crank it up higher as the instructions are for beginners—not for people as fit as us.

I turned it right up to its maximum, 6500 metres, and continued to sleep well and feel OK, even though the oxygen saturation in my blood was around 72 per cent. But then, after about three weeks of this intensive oxygen starvation, my immune system absolutely crashed and I got a kidney infection. I also managed to get a hypoxic brain concussion, which basically means that your brain isn't getting enough oxygen so the cells start to die off. I had to spend a month recovering and was back to square one as I had sensitised my body to altitude instead of desensitising it.

This was possibly the least ideal build-up I could have had for what promised to be the most challenging race of my life.

Flying out to India I still had a lot of pain, but nothing was going to stop me. On that flight, I was incredibly scared. Before I left, people had been telling me that I was going to die or get really sick from the altitude. It completely freaked me out. But then I realised that I was the one in control of whether that happened or not. I had a serious talk with myself about how far I was prepared to go to get to the finish line and I did my best to mentally prepare myself for the battle to come. I knew that to succeed I had to deal with the obstacles, be flexible and prepare—the rest was in the lap of the gods.

From the moment I was invited to enter this race, I knew that it would test me in new and unimaginable ways. The great unknowns for me were the altitude, the freezing temperatures and the environment. The Himalayas are a long way from my beloved Mount Taranaki.

It took me 35 hours to get from Auckland to Leh, in India's Jammu and Kashmir province. Leh stands at an altitude of 3500 metres and is home to a hardy 27,000 residents. It would also be my home for the next two weeks as I spent time trying to acclimatise to the high altitude. I don't normally have the luxury of spending that long at a destination before an event, but I knew that this one was going to be super tough and I needed to give myself every opportunity to adjust before starting the race.

Flying into the town was absolutely spectacular. Leh is in the region of Ladakh, which is also known as Little Tibet. The view from the plane made it pretty clear to me why. It was only on seeing the Himalayas for the first time that I truly realised the massive scale of what I was about to take on.

One of the first things I noticed in Leh was the huge army presence. This is largely due to the fact that Jammu and Kashmir border both China and Pakistan. All three countries dispute the legal ownership of the region and this has led to intense cross-border clashes over the years. While most of the population of the area are Muslim, the Ladakh region has a strong Buddhist influence and the town is dominated by the now ruined Leh Palace, that used to be home to the royal family of Ladakh.

Speaking of palaces, I soon managed to find my way to my hotel. It was nowhere near a palace, but it was clean and I was happy to have somewhere to rest my travel-weary bones. The hotel's electricity supply was sporadic, at best, so there was only cold water for bathing. That's bad enough in a temperate climate, but up there in the mountains, it was freezing. That said, I was almost used to it after all the post-run ice baths I've endured over the years.

My first day in Leh I felt pretty dazed and swollen from flying. Most of my day was spent finding my way around town and going on a mission to find some toilet paper. The people in the town were really laidback, except for the army guys. It was easy to see that they weren't to be messed with. Unlike other parts of the world, I found I felt quite safe out walking by myself and when I went into shops no-one hassled me, they just left me to browse and find what I wanted.

While on my mission to find toilet paper, which was successful, by the way, I also managed to find a couple of shops selling beautiful local gemstones. In my other life, when I'm not running mad missions, I have my own jewellery business. Wherever I am in the world, I always try to find local gems and artisan jewellery to take home with me. In Leh there was an abundance of it and I could have filled my suitcases several times over.

That first day I also met Kunal, a local climbing guide and part of the organising team for the race. It was great to be able to sit down and talk to him about how best to cope with acclimatising to the altitude.

Kunal told me that while he was mapping the course, he experienced sandstorms, snowstorms, rain and wind, and all within a few short hours. The weather up there can change in an instant, which was going to add to the challenges the athletes would face.

After my meeting with Kunal, I visited a local Buddhist site and spun a mani, or prayer wheel, while chanting the traditional Buddhist mantra or prayer 'Om mani padme hum', which calls on generosity, ethics, patience, diligence, renunciation and wisdom. I figured I'd need all of these things to get me through the next few weeks so I really hoped the mantra would work for me.

The following day, I got to talk to Mum on the phone, which was wonderful. I always miss home as soon as I'm away, but especially so when I'm travelling in third-world countries. It just makes me appreciate every little thing that I take for granted at home, like flushing toilets and electricity.

The same day, I had my first meeting with my crewmember and sponsor Sunny Grewal. Sunny is originally from India but now lives in New Plymouth where he owns the restaurant India Today. The pair of us soon set about putting together a plan for the next few days, which largely consisted of checking out some of the route of the race to see how my lungs would cope and doing some sightseeing.

Even with the homesickness, I adjusted pretty quickly to life in Leh. Well, most of me did—it took my lungs a while to start coping. Puffing for breath when you're sitting doing nothing is a very weird experience, made all the more scary with the knowledge that I was going to head up another 2000 metres and run for two days solid. I didn't know how I was going to do it, but then I didn't know how I was going to walk across the Libyan Desert with a 35-kilogram pack on my back and I managed that. I could manage this, surely . . . surely. What is it that I always preach about believing in yourself and scaring yourself regularly?

During the first week, I didn't do a hell of a lot except try to get my breathing under control. I spent quite a bit of time exploring Leh. For a small town, it was a pretty chaotic place made up of a mix of staunch Indian army soldiers, Buddhist monks, hippy tourists, druggies and hardcore mountain climbers.

My first experience of the course we'd be running came when Sunny and I took a taxi up the Khardung La pass, which we'd be running over on the first morning of the race. It was

5400 metres above sea level and just walking around up there was a mission. That said, it was good to get out there and get an idea of where I'd be running as it helped to calm my fear a little bit.

Sunny and I also did a mission up the second pass of the race, Tanglang La ('La' means 'pass' in Tibetan). It was pretty tough even driving up there so I tried hard not to think about having to run up it. At 5359 metres above sea level, I knew Tanglang La was going to be the biggest test of the race for me. Even though it's slightly lower than Khardung La, it comes so much later in the race that I know when I reach it, the impact of the altitude will be intensified by fatigue and lack of sleep.

Adding to my worries about getting organised for the race was the fact that I was not only going to be running it but also making a documentary about it. Near the end of my first week in Leh, I got word that the cameraman who had signed up to film it had pulled out. I couldn't believe it. His tickets were booked and his crew fee had been paid. I was really disappointed but another one of my crew members, Chris Ord, who is a Melbourne-based writer, managed to pull off a miracle and find another cameraman keen to have the adventure of his life.

The only problem now was arranging visas and changing air tickets for our new camera guy, Luke McNee. This was all stuff I really didn't need to be worrying about but Rajat Chauhan, the race director, and the team from Air Asia, who the crew were flying with, were absolutely brilliant. Somehow they managed to move mountains and make sure that Luke was on the right plane to get there in time.

After a week in Leh, Sunny's brother-in-law, Rana, joined us. The three of us went up to Khardung La again. Every day I tried to push myself a little harder and this day was no exception. I managed to run (well, walk, really) 10.5 kilometres up to the top of the pass and then 5 kilometres down the other side. Even though I vomited on the way up the road, I still managed to keep going. Again my lungs were screaming for air the whole way up and it was impossible to eat. Even drinking water, which I had to do every three minutes due to the dryness of the air, was difficult and I had to spend the next ten steps trying to get my breath back. This was a really new experience.

Running this road for the first time gave me a warning of just how difficult it was going to be in race conditions. Not because of the landscape or the climb but because of the numerous trucks and jeeps that were on the road. Every vehicle that went past me was belching out full-on black diesel smoke which, combined with the lack of oxygen, made me really nauseous and gave me terrible headaches. Add to that the fact that many of the drivers seemed to have a death wish and it's no wonder I got pretty scared.

While I was running up Khardung La, a couple of rock avalanches came down over the road. While it was kind of scary, it also meant that I knew that avalanches were a possibility and I could plan for them happening. Someone on my crew was going to have to don a backpack with water and continue with me until the rocks were cleared and the car could carry on. Snow and rock avalanches are a regular occurrence there.

When I finally reached the top of the pass, Sunny and I stopped for a beautiful cup of chai. Delicious, although not so appealing when I started to feel like I was going to vomit it back up again about 5 kilometres into the run back down the mountain. At that point I called it a day. When I got back to my hotel I managed a quick wash under the cold tap, rinsed my clothes and collapsed into bed feeling really sick. Since when did a little 15-kilometre run annihilate me? Never!

The altitude was still really getting to me so I sent a quick email to my exercise physiologist, Dr Reginald O'Hara, who works for the US Air Force. I outlined my symptoms to him and asked how I'd know when the altitude sickness was getting really serious. After all, I was used to pushing my body to the limits in hot conditions, but in the cold and altitude I wasn't so sure how to read my symptoms.

In his reply, Dr O'Hara told me to monitor my oxygen saturation levels and not to get too worried unless my saturation was below 90 per cent for any period of time. (Little did he know that it was consistently below 90 per cent on ground lower than I'd be climbing to.) He said that from my symptoms it sounded like I had mild altitude sickness and that I should rest for a bit. This put my mind at ease and I decided that sightseeing would be the order of the day for the next day.

One of the great things about having Indian crew members for a race like this was that Sunny and Rana were able to organise all the things that I could never have managed myself. I was particularly happy when they managed to arrange a local SIM card for my phone—that would usually only be available to local people because of the tight military restrictions in place. This meant that I could talk to my mum again. The great thing about Mum being at the other end of the phone was that I could stop being brave and have a wee meltdown. I knew Mum would understand that and it really helped. I've always felt that I have to be upbeat around my crews and that I can't show weakness with them, so having an outlet for my fears was very soothing.

While I was talking to her she told me that she'd recently met a woman in New Plymouth who had worked in Leh as a vet. Apparently, her main job had been treating the many hundreds of wild dogs in the area. I've since found out that Fiona Chapman and her colleague Oliver Walkinton are part of a group called Vets without Borders. Every year they go to Leh and trap, treat and sterilise hundreds of wild dogs. It never ceases to amaze me where Taranaki folk end up. The job these vets do is a thankless and never-ending task but they are people who are contributing in a way that has tangible results.

After talking to Mum, I fell into bed and slept really soundly. That was until my dreams were interrupted by a huge crash and the tinkling of glass. I woke with a start wondering if there was someone in my room. I was scared but too tired to get up and check it out. Eventually, I went back to sleep and awoke in the morning to find my room covered in broken glass. A window in my bedroom had smashed but I suspect it was the result of shoddy workmanship rather than anything more sinister. It sometimes seemed that everything in Leh was held together by chewing gum and sticky tape.

After a broken night's sleep, I was happy to take the doctor's advice about slowing down for a bit. Sunny had arranged for one of his friends to take me sightseeing for the day. Sunny's friend Arjun was in the army and was not meant to be seen in the company of foreign nationals. That didn't stop him organising a brilliant day out for all of us. His hospitality was second to none.

First stop on our tour was Stok Gompa, 15 kilometres south of Leh—gompa means monastery. It stands at the base of the over 6000-metre peak of Stok Mountain. It is one of the residences of the banished Ladakhi royal family and also houses the family museum. I was in awe of the delicate jewellery work on show and the elaborate turquoise headdresses worn by the royals on special occasions. I looked down the list at the long line of kings and queens reaching back hundreds of years and noted that most did not live past the age of 25, so harsh are the conditions up here.

Next stop was an incredible monastery with over 300 lamas in residence. The temples and shrines to Buddha were amazingly intricate and colourful. Here, each family in the surrounding 60 villages must present a male child to the monastery to become a lama. There were lots of little boys wandering around in the traditional burgundy-coloured monastic robes. I couldn't help but wonder what their lives must be like—a life of dedication to their religion and owning no material wealth, only spiritual wealth. It seemed to me to be a harsh life but these boys were all smiling and seemed to be really happy kids.

After a hot and wild ride in the jeep, we arrived at our second monastery of the day. The Matho Gompa was over 600 years old but it was the new addition that was just three years old that wowed me. The shrine to Buddha there was magnificent and as colourful as a rainbow.

After spinning the prayer wheels in the hope of some help during the race, we were treated to a very special lunch with a local family who had obviously been cooking for hours. They had carried the picnic, including carpets and pots, some 2 kilometres from their home to lay it out in the shade of a beautiful tree next to a river.

Before lunch, I had a refreshing wash in the river to get rid of the dust from the roads. We were then offered the most delicious apricot juice I've ever tasted followed by some serious beer. This lovely family had prepared a feast fit for a king. I ate gratefully and hungrily, enjoying the unusual flavours of the new cuisine. The hospitality shown to me as a stranger was touching for this little Kiwi a long way from home. It was a wonderful day and it gave me a chance to briefly forget the immensity of the challenge that lay ahead.

The following day the rest of the runners and their crews arrived from Delhi. I'm glad I got up here before them as I really don't think nine days would have been enough time for me to acclimatise.

It was great to be reunited with Sam Gash. After the adventures we'd had in the Gobi and the Sahara, Sam and I have really bonded. Also in the line-up for the race were Molly Sheridan, who ran the race the previous year but didn't complete it, ultrarunning legend Sharon Gayter from the UK, Aussie runner Jason Rita and legendary Badwater and Arrowhead 135 champ Ray Sanchez.

It's always a bit strange when the contestants in a race like this first get together. We all spend a bit of time quietly sizing each other up before getting into the serious business of swapping plans and talking about the race to come.

With the rest of the runners here, I received the good news that Luke, the cameraman, had his visas and was on a flight to India. After all the work that had gone into getting the documentary team together, it would have been a real shame if we'd had to pull the pin at the last minute.

My delight at Luke being on his way was soon tempered with some really bad news. My main man, Sunny, had got word from home that one of his family members was very ill. He was sad to have to leave me and I was sad to see him go, but health and family must always come first. Sunny had looked after me like a big brother and I was so very grateful for all his help throughout my time in Leh.

Before he left, Sunny arranged for his brother-in-law, Rana, to take his place on my crew. Rana had been with us all week but didn't speak much English. Still, I was happy not to have to get to know a new crew member this late in the day. We also got another Indian driver, Venkat, allocated to us and we decided to pay extra to get a second vehicle during the race because we had so much gear. An extra vehicle would also mean our cameraman could run ahead getting good footage while the crew stayed with me.

With all of the runners now in Leh, we had our first medical briefing. It was kind of weird to have seven runners and five doctors. But the news that two tourists had recently died from altitude sickness on their first evening in Leh made us all realise just how necessary such intensive medical supervision would be as we were going to be pushing ourselves through extreme conditions. The doctors would be monitoring all of us throughout the lead-up to the race and during the race itself.

My ninth day in Leh was very exciting. I woke with the birds, excited in the knowledge that the next of my crew members, Chris Ord, was due to arrive on a flight at 6.25 a.m. The weather was bright and cool, which made me feel even better.

Even though he'd just done an epic flight from Australia, Chris wasn't interested in my advice to take some down time. He was bouncing and ready for action. When I told him I was going to head up the 580 steps to Shanti Stupa, a beautiful white-domed Buddhist shrine above the city, Chris was dead keen to join me, but the race doctors told him to sit tight. It was good advice given he hadn't had time to adjust to the altitude.

After my trek up to Shanti Stupa, I had to attend a medical check-up. Even after a week of acclimatising, my oxygen saturation level was only 90 per cent while resting. Given Dr O'Hara's advice I was a bit concerned, but the race doctors reckoned it was OK. All vital signs were checked and noted including weight, blood pressure, haemoglobin and pulse.

The medical crew were from Delaware in the United States and they were very thorough. They were doing research into the time it takes for the body to adapt to altitude in trained athletes as compared to the crew members. Most of us took part in the study as the results could be very helpful for athletes taking on this kind of adventure in the future.

Two days after Chris's arrival, the rest of my team flew in to Leh. Luke McNee flew in at 6 a.m. and neither Chris nor I had ever met him before. We just looked for the white guy with a huge amount of luggage and found him quite easily! Then at 10 a.m. it was back out to the airport to pick up my New Plymouth trainer, Josh Paurini. It was Josh's first time out of New Zealand and he'd done the mammoth flight from New Zealand to Leh straight through without any stopovers. Any normal person would have been absolutely shattered, but Josh just took it all in his stride.

With the team all in place, we set off to gather supplies and food. Leh has heaps of tiny shops selling a very limited supply of products. In order to get everything we needed we had to go to what felt like nearly every shop in town. But at the end of our mission we had one seat, two gas cartridges for the cooker, two packets of 2-minute noodles, four packets of soup, some tissues, some chewing gum, a jar of apricot marmalade, quarter of a kilo of almonds, a jar of Nutella and some crackers. Enough to feed six people for six days? I doubt it, somehow!

One of the things I love about doing a race like this is getting to know the other runners. One morning, I spent some time with Sharon Gayter. She and I shared our war stories about battling asthma. She told me she had run 42 kilometres downhill the previous day and had trouble with her breathing. She said her inhalers didn't work properly at altitude. It must have been scary for her given the exhaust fumes coupled with the altitude. It meant that the race doctors realised they needed to organise nebulisers for both of us in case we needed them during the race.

With that knowledge safely under my belt, Chris, Venkat, Rana and I piled into the van and headed up to Khardung La pass. It was Chris's first time up there. We left Josh and Luke behind as they had only arrived the day before and it would have been too dangerous to take them up any higher that soon.

With Luke staying down in Leh, Chris had to play camera-man for the day. I was bit worried when he told me he'd had an upset stomach the night before but he assured me he was OK. As I headed up the pass, he jumped out of the van and ran beside me to get some footage. It wasn't long before he had a real headache from the altitude.

Once again, I had trouble with my asthma on the road. The strong wind and the vehicle fumes made it difficult to get my breath at the best of times anyway and I struggled to get my breathing under control. As had happened on my previous run up the pass, a rock avalanche came down and blocked the road. Rana and Chris grabbed the water bottles and stuck with me, while Venkat waited in the van until the road was cleared. It wasn't long before Chris had to head back to the van as his headache was getting worse as the day wore on.

That left Rana running with me. Given he wasn't a runner, he did really well in keeping pace with me for 4 kilometres. That might not sound like much but every kilometre up there is equivalent to about 10 kilometres at sea level.

I plodded on to the top of the pass completing just 12.5 kilometres. I immediately went and stuck my finger in the oxygen-saturation monitoring machine that I had with me. At sea level, the normal saturation is 98 per cent. Prolonged levels below 90 per cent are considered to be dangerous. At the top of the Khardung La, mine was just 79 per cent. I knew that if it got any lower than 72 per cent I'd really be in trouble, so we stayed on top for a good hour trying to use the time to acclimatise.

I still couldn't get my head around how I was possibly going to run/walk/crawl 222 kilometres in these conditions in just a few days' time when doing just 12 kilometres was knocking me for six, and doing just 1 or 2 kilometres was dealing it to my crew. I just kept praying and trying to think positive and taking it slow. Incomprehensible was the word of the moment.

Once we got back down to Leh, I had to go out on a supply mission because all the shops and restaurants were going to be closed the following day. The reason for the closure was the first anniversary of the disastrous floods that had hit the city the previous August. Flash floods triggered by heavy overnight rain killed at least 193 people and left thousands more homeless. According to the Indian Meteorological Bureau, Leh received its average monthly rainfall within 24 hours. I can only imagine what the carnage must have been like.

With everything in Leh closed for the day, the crew and I decided to head up to Tanglang La for another practice run. But before we went, we sat down and had a long briefing from Molly Sheridan, who had attempted the race the previous year. She managed the first 120 kilometres of the 222-kilometre race before pulling out.

Sharing her experiences with us proved to be invaluable when it came to our planning. She told us that her local crew had left her near the top of the pass and carried on up to the top. They had broken the cardinal rule of crewing—never leave your runner. Worse than that though, when they got to the top of the pass they decided to wind up the windows of their car and have a sleep. They both nearly died.

According to race organiser, Kunal, when the medics got to them, the pair had oxygen saturation levels of just 30 per cent. Poor Molly was, by that stage, severely dehydrated and left without anyone crewing for her. She ended up in hospital on an intravenous drip, all because her crew members had left her.

After Molly spoke, the race director, Rajat Chauhan, also talked to us about the previous year's race. He had accompanied Mark Cockbain—the only runner to complete the race—up the last pass. At the bottom of the pass, Mark decided to stop to cook up some soup but, because of the altitude, cooking with gas takes much longer. By the time his soup was warm enough to eat, Mark had started to suffer from hypothermia. Rajat said he had no idea how Mark kept going. Apparently, the last pass took him ten hours of running through the freezing night to get over.

Rajat reckoned Mark had been completely delirious for much of the climb. It must have been difficult for Rajat, as a doctor, to find a balance between letting Mark finish the race and being concerned for his safety.

After hearing both their stories, all of the crews and runners were bombarding both Rajat and Molly with questions. Hearing tales like these made it even harder for me to feel safe about the epic mission I was about to take on, but I'd come this far and there was no way I was going to back down.

That day we had our first outing as a complete team and the first altitude excursion for Josh and Luke. While driving up one of the passes, we had a particularly close encounter with a family of donkeys when our driver decided to overtake an army truck at the same time as they were crossing the road.

The driver slammed on the brakes just in time, throwing us all out of our deep altitude-induced slumbers. Terrifying.

Even after our near-death experience, I was feeling quite good so I decided to run the 12 kilometres up to the top of the pass. At one point while I was running I had 30 huge army trucks pass me, all bellowing black smoke out of their exhausts. From then on, I had to fight with asthma. I would just get it under control then have to sip some water, and each sip caused my bronchial tubes to shut down on me. It took a lot of concentration and calming thoughts to stop the panic taking over completely.

While running up the pass, I tested out whether I could eat anything while going uphill. Near the top I managed to get down the sum total of one lolly and one peanut. Not a great calorific intake given the extreme nature of the climb I was doing. It made me wonder how the hell I was going to be able to get enough kilojoules in to get me through the whole race.

After a brief stop at the top of the pass, a big group hug and some filming, we headed back down to Leh. The total trip took nine hours so we had a long trip back to Leh. While still en route we pulled out some of the food we had bought the day before, including a pizza. This turned out to be a very bad idea. Josh soon started feeling sick, Venkat wasn't feeling so good and I had to get the driver to stop the car so I could get out and vomit. Car sickness + altitude + crazy driving + pizza is not a good equation.

When we got down to the nearest village there was a ceremony being held for the anniversary of the flood. The locals were giving out fried bread and tea and happily invited us to join in their commemorations. Their hospitality was lovely.

The following day, I woke at 4 a.m. with bad stomach cramps. I had planned to spend the day running again but

I was so tired and weak that I could barely walk up to the Shanti Stupa. By the time I got back to my room, all hell broke loose with my tummy and I had to just go to bed and sleep. In the meantime, the boys went out on a shopping excursion to top up our food supplies for the race.

Given I was meant to be racing in two days' time, I was a bit scared that I wouldn't shake this bug. The race doctors were onto it though and quickly got me a course of antibiotics. I knew that Chris's tummy troubles had cleared up quickly so I really hoped mine would, too.

After a good sleep during the day, I felt well enough to go into town to do some filming with the boys. Chris was interviewing me as we walked through the chaotic streets near the town's market. While we walked and talked, Josh and Venkat kept an eye on Chris, who was walking backwards, to make sure he didn't get hit or walk into anything. On the streets, there were donkeys, wild dogs, carts, beggars, too many cars and heaps of people. It was crazy and we all had to be really careful. As we turned a corner, Josh got distracted and Chris got sideswiped by a car. It was bloody scary but, thankfully, there was no damage to Chris or the car. And it made for some damn good footage for our doco!

The next morning I got woken at 5 a.m. by the sounds of the worst dog fight I have ever heard. It was absolutely horrific and made me think about those New Plymouth vets who give up their time to come up here and look after these poor creatures.

After my early wake-up, I decided to spend the day packing and sorting out all my gear. The boys went sightseeing at the nearby Thiksey Gompa. I would have loved to have gone but I was here to race and I needed to focus on getting everything right for the run. Venkat and Josh came back early but Luke and Chris continued on up Tanglang La pass with some of the other runners so they could film them. Given it was a nine-hour trip there and back, I was impressed by their dedication. For me though it was all about rest and recovery as race day was only a few days away.

Two days before the race we moved up to Khardung Village, which was at an altitude of 4200 metres. It gave us all a chance to acclimatise to the higher altitude a bit, which was great. Up until this point I'd been totally freaking out about the race. When we got out to the site, the tents weren't there and there was nowhere to stay. We were assured that the tents were on their way, but it didn't really ease our concerns.

Never one to sit back and do nothing, Ray Sanchez went to a tiny village nearby and managed to convince a local woman to rent him a room. We were all quite jealous. He then invited Molly and her crew to stay in the room with him—and we're talking a tiny room with a concrete floor. I decided that if this woman was going to let Ray and Molly stay, she might have another room for me and my crew. She did, but she wasn't that keen on renting it to us. In the end, we managed to convince her and we all piled in.

The room upstairs had a beautiful view out across the Himalayas. It was really special. Josh had his guitar with him so he got it out and led a bit of a singalong. It was actually quite relaxing.

The tents finally arrived late that night. Where the campsite was meant to be set up, near the village, had been flooded out and the site was moved a couple of kilometres up the road. All the other athletes and their crews headed up there. We decided to stay in our lodgings, even though it meant being stuck a couple of kilometres away from the rest of the group. To get food, we all had to make the trek over to the camp. The cooks were brilliant so we didn't mind the inconvenience of it too much.

On the second day out at Khardung, everyone was focused on sorting out all their gear. We had all ordered cars to carry our crew and gear during the race. The cars were due to come from Leh at midday on the day before the race. It got to nine at night and the cars still hadn't arrived. Talk about panic. We were due to be starting the race first thing in the morning and it takes hours to set a crew car up properly. Everything has to have its place. You need to be able to access everything in the car quickly when you're crewing on a race like this. If you need bandages, food, water, inhalers, a spare tyre, whatever, you've got to know where it is and how to get to it quickly. And we had not one but two crew cars—one for the documentary team and one for the rest of the crew. We were fast running out of time to get them set up properly.

That evening we were all sitting around in one of the tents eating dinner and waiting for the cars to arrive. All of a sudden a gust of wind came up out of nowhere and within seconds there was a full-on hurricane. You could see the storm rolling in over the Himalayas. It was wild weather and watching the cloud formations coming up was absolutely freaky.

One minute we were sitting there happily eating dinner and the next minute the tent had fallen down on top of us. We were all scrambling to get out and running around trying to hold everything down. At the same time, we were all trying to hang onto our plates of food because we knew it would be the last decent meal we'd be able to get down for a while!

Samantha and I had already finished our main meals and we were onto dessert. There we were trying to hold onto to the tent with one hand while grabbing onto chunks of chocolate cake with the other.

While the tent was blowing around, I couldn't help but think, 'Thank bloody goodness we're in our little room while the rest of these poor bastards have to spend the night under canvas in the middle of this crazy weather.' Mind you, I was also conscious of the fact that the storm might last into the next day and I didn't want to have to run in conditions like that.

Up until that point, I'd felt quite lethargic because of all the fear and waiting around. For some reason the storm gave me a massive adrenaline boost that just changed my whole feeling about the race. I was buzzed out and couldn't wait to get started. The wilder nature is the more alive I feel. It woke me up completely.

That night I went to bed thinking, well, there's no way out now. I had to forget all the dangers, all the fear-mongering and the scary stories. I knew that I had to go through it. When the alarm went off at four in the morning, I had that momentary feeling of wondering where I was until the realisation dawned on. This was it. This was D-Day. Oh shit. All the boys got up and were rushing around trying to finish packing the crew cars that had finally arrived at ten o'clock the previous night.

I stayed in my sleeping bag for as long as possible, knowing that I wouldn't be lying down again for a couple of days— well, hoping I wouldn't be lying down again for a couple of days. Then I started to get all my race kit on. It's quite a ritual for me. I sit there quietly and braid my hair. I put my Injinji toe socks on, then The North Face gear, and then I put my race bib on. The last thing I put on is my game face. At that point the shutters come down and I'm completely focused on what I have to do.

The race started 11 kilometres outside of Khardung Village, effectively in the middle of nowhere, to make sure the course was 222 kilometres long. Sitting in the car driving down to the start line at 6 a.m., the guys could see the fear in my eyes. They did everything they could to keep me focused and on task.

When we got to the start line, we all had to be medically checked and weighed. Then before we knew it, we were lining up at the start line. All this support, infrastructure and effort just for six runners. Amazing.

Then the gun went and we were off.

Heading up the first pass, Khardung La, where I'd done so much of my training, I just wanted to go slowly and conserve my energy. I knew that if I blew out on the first pass, I'd be in dire straits for the second pass later in the race, Tanglang La. For the first pass, I was pretty fresh and going up to that altitude for the first time with fresh legs and lungs. For the second pass, which is actually lower than Khardung La, I knew I'd be fatigued and sleep deprived.

All the other runners seemed to take off really fast except for me and Molly Sheridan. I figured that as Molly had been out there and done it before, she knew what she was doing so I stayed back with her. Ray Sanchez and Sharon Gayter went out like absolute bullets. Winning La Ultra 2011 was always going to be a race between the two of them and the rivalry between them was palpable right from the start. There was no way I was even going to contemplate trying to keep up with them. Jason Rita, who is a really strong runner, too, was just behind them. Sam Gash, who was still pretty inexperienced at this level, took off quickly, too, which surprised me a bit, but if there's one thing I know about Sam it's that she's bloody determined.

Hanging out down the back were me and Molly. About 20 kilometres up the pass, there was a military station that had a little tea hut. There they supplied us with hot water. The boys stopped and made me some 2-minute noodles. I didn't really want to eat them but the crew tried to force them into me. It was my own fault as I'd told them it was crucial that they get food into me before I got too knackered to eat.

Because it was quite cold I was actually quite hungry, which is unusual for me when I'm out running. I was feeling quite strong and I'd passed Sam Gash a few kilometres back as she was starting to feel the effects of the altitude and already had a massive headache. We ran together for a bit before I moved on.

Anyway, I started eating the noodles the boys had cooked up for me and I was really enjoying them. I put my hand up for a second cup of noodles, which they duly brought me as I kept walking. I felt like I was being a bit greedy but thought I'd get as many kilojoules into my system while I still felt like it. With noodles in hand, the boys went on ahead. I got around the next corner and then I realised the second cup had been a big mistake. Before long I'd thrown the whole lot up and was back to square one. I was pissed off because I'd really enjoyed the noodles, but the air was just getting thinner and thinner making it really hard to hold anything down.

After that I just stuck to sucking on high-energy sweets. Trying to suck on one of those while you're effectively breathing through a straw is really not easy. Every time I'd take a swig of water, I had to virtually stop to drink it and get enough oxygen to carry on.

I took it really gently up Khardung La. But as the day wore on the diesel trucks came out in force. Unfortunately, we'd timed our run to coincide with several convoys of army trucks crossing the pass. Military convoys were an unfortunate and unavoidable feature of the race. The Khardung La is on the road between India and Pakistan. Given the area was so politically unstable, the military presence was massive and I felt like nearly every army truck and soldier in the whole region drove past me on the way up the pass that day.

Each convoy would be made up of about thirty trucks. The road was incredibly narrow with a massive drop on one side. It's two-lane traffic the whole way but there's really only one lane. These guys didn't give a toss about this group of mad runners trying to run up their road. I couldn't help but feel that if they'd knocked me off the edge, they wouldn't even stop. There was so little space on the road that it was absolutely treacherous.

At one point on the road, Chris came up to me and shoved me against the cliff. Just as he did it, a convoy of trucks came roaring past. I hadn't even noticed them coming but if he hadn't done that, I'd have been splattered. Then just ahead of me, they all ended up in a traffic jam, so after nearly being killed by these thirty-odd trucks, I had to run past them all. Inevitably, as soon as they got moving again, they all passed me again. At least this time we knew what to expect, and Chris and I cowered against the cliff until they'd gone past.

The crazy driving wasn't the only risk. The diesel fumes soon started to get to me. None of these trucks had any kind of filter on them and they were pumping out black smoke at my eye level. Because it was at high altitude, the fumes don't dissipate like they would nearer sea level. They just hang around and the whole mountain stinks of diesel all the time. So much for running in the pristine Himalayan environment—I reckon I'd have had to deal with less pollution if I was running through some of the world's most populated cities.

Further up the pass we had a big stone avalanche that I had to climb over. These avalanches come down on a regular basis up there and I was just lucky not to have been hit by one. The crew car had to wait for the road to be cleared while I ran on ahead with Chris. I knew that the year before Mark Cockbain had had to contend with snow avalanches, too. I was thankful for the small mercy that I only had to deal with rocks.

Eventually I got to the top of Khardung La and I was feeling not too bad. I had a bit of a headache from the altitude but I was OK. At the top of the pass, there's a sign that reads:

Suggestions for Visitors at Khardung La Top
1. Always have a cheerful attitude.
2. Contact nearest medical detachment on having headache, nausea, vomiting, chest pain, cough, redness and swelling of fingers. There is a medical detachment at Khardung La Top.
3. Avoid using toilets on Khardung La Top due to environmental reasons please use toilets at South Pullu.
4. Avoid running and moving too fast at Khardung La Top. Please don't exert too much.
5. Avoid consumption of alcohol and smoking.
6. Do not stay for long durations at Khardung La Top (ideal time is 30 minutes) since you have gained approximately 7000 feet in two hours time. Height of Leh is 11300 ft, while height of K Top is at 18380 ft. Thank you.

I'm pretty sure that whoever painted that sign never banked on six people running over the pass. I wish it had only taken me two hours to get up there but I was happy that I was able to obey at least one of the suggestions, the fourth on the list—'Avoid running and moving too fast at Khardung La Top. Please don't exert too much.'

Heading back down the other side, I just tried to go as quickly as possible. The key piece of advice I can give anyone who is running at altitude is get down, get down, get down. Don't waste time up there.

From the top, I sent one of the crew cars down lower and kept the bare minimum of crew up with me. The reason for this was that I didn't want any of the crew to get altitude sickness from spending too much time up near the top of the pass. I wanted them to be fresh for the second pass to come. They waited for me at the next control point about 20 kilometres down the mountain.

As I started heading down the other side of the pass, I realised that I couldn't even run downhill. I had thought that even though uphill was tough and I had to walk it, downhill would be easier and I'd be able to run it. Turns out I was wrong. My breathing was so laboured that I had to walk the first 5 kilometres downhill. As I got a bit further down the pass where there was more oxygen available, I was finally able to start running. From there I managed to run most of the 20-odd kilometres down into Leh.

There was another military checkpoint about halfway down the pass where the race doctors were stationed. They checked in all the runners, weighed us all and made sure we were OK. I was having quite bad asthma attacks so at this point I had to use a nebuliser to get my medication into my lungs. My fingers were a bit numb from not having enough oxygen in the body but otherwise I was feeling OK.

I arrived in Leh at about eight o'clock at night. After running on what was pretty much a single-lane road all day, it was quite a shock to suddenly be faced with five lanes of traffic. The way they drive over there is just chaos and there were no footpaths to keep me safe. I freaked out and was convinced I was going to get run over. Thankfully I had my high-visibility vest on and, because it was night-time, I also had lights on me.

Two of my crew ran along either side of me and protected me from the traffic. Venkat and Rana guided me through the traffic but, even with them at my side, I still nearly got side-swiped by a bus while trying to cross the road. I couldn't help thinking that this was not what I came to the Himalayas for!

There's one road that goes from Leh to Manali, in neighbouring Himachal Pradesh. It's the main road linking Ladakh with the rest of India so there was a hell of a lot of traffic on it in the early hours of the evening. The three of us were running along, trying very hard to keep out of the way of the traffic.

Having survived the traffic, we kept on running out into the night. Ten kilometres from Leh there was meant to be a big depot where my crew could get food and restock our water. We had also been promised Indian drivers from this depot on because we weren't meant to be driving on these crazy roads. Once we got to where the depot was meant to be, we found that it was about 600 metres off the road. There was no way I was going to add even 50 metres to my race even if it meant food and water. My big plan to have a break there went out the window, which was really disappointing.

A couple of the crew were hoping to have a rest there as they'd planned to work in shifts. There were a couple of beds there but there were about 100 people wanting them so it was a real scrap for them to even get a lie down.

The most tricky thing was that the new drivers who were supposed to be supplied by the race organisers weren't there. I was fortunate that I had my own crew as well as my Indian crew so I always had someone with me. Ray Sanchez, who only had an Indian crew, suddenly found that he had no driver.

I was also lucky that I had two cars and both Venkat and Rana with me. They took turns driving, but without the

Indian drivers, it meant that for a while we were down to one crew car. Venkat ended up driving for really long hours on the most dangerous of roads, which was a bit scary. Foreigners aren't allowed to drive these roads, partly because the roads are so dangerous and partly due to the tight military controls in the region.

I ran through the night and my guys were absolutely brilliant. They ran with me and talked to me all night, which was what kept me going. They told me stories, they held my hand as I kept dropping off to sleep, and they made sure I kept putting one foot in front of the other while I tortured myself trying to stay awake. The boys got me through those horrible hours of the early morning.

In those early hours, I made it to the village of Upshi where I turned off the main road and headed towards Tanglang La. During the floods the previous year, Upshi had been hit particularly hard with numerous villagers being killed. The flooding had also washed away a large stretch of the road and it was still being rebuilt. There were people crouched on the side of the roads, rebuilding it by hand. Armed with small hammers in the heat of the high-altitude desert, they were smashing rocks to make gravel to repair the roads. I really felt for them as I ran through their washed-out valley. The devastation in the villages along the way was still visible with water marks sometimes metres above our heads.

After the turn-off up towards Tanglang La, I found myself running through a river valley on an almost washed-out narrow road. It was a bit like running through a canyon. Whenever you get a landscape like that it funnels the heat and it absolutely cooks you. I was up over 4000 metres so the sun was hotter than usual anyway. Going through that part of the race was the low point for me. I had altitude sickness and heat stroke—I wasn't in great condition to start heading up the second big pass of the race. The lower part of Tanglang La was about 30 kilometres of slow climbing in the heat. It was awful.

Running along the road, Rana was by my side and all of a sudden I blanked out and ended up in a crumpled heap on the ground. Chris came running over and picked me up. The pair of them managed to get me back over to the car and I lay down for a few minutes. They put some cold water on my head and did their best to cool me down.

Once I'd cooled down a bit, I got back out there. Chris came out and stayed with me all afternoon through that horrible heat and the slow climb. There was meant to be another major camp before hitting the pass proper. I was planning to have a bit of a rest there, too. I kept moving and it didn't come and it didn't come. I finally got there at about three in the afternoon. I had an hour's rest there but it was like trying to rest in a toilet. It was horrible but I was desperate for a break so I didn't care. I lay down on the concrete floor and slept for an hour. I also got some hot food into me, which helped me to feel a bit better.

At that point, I was thinking there was no way I could keep going up. The whole way I'd been terrified of the second pass. The way I was feeling with heat stroke and nausea, knowing that I had to climb up to 5400 metres again with night-time approaching, I was thinking there was no frigging way I could do it. But I didn't want to say anything negative to my crew so I decided to go down fighting.

Chris and Josh stayed at the camp for a rest because they were just about as knackered as me. I went on ahead with Venkat and Rana. It surprised me when I got back out there that it had started to cool off. For the next few hours, the temperature was pleasant as I was climbing steadily up this pass.

I started to think, 'Maybe I can do it . . . ' But then I'd think that it was another 30-odd kilometres to the top, which was a bloody long way and anything could happen.

A few hours later, Chris and Josh caught up to me and it was a real buzz for me to be reunited with them. I was starting to flag but they told me that I was way further up the pass than they thought I would be. That gave me a bit of a kick along. Again, I thought, 'Maybe I can, maybe I can . . . ' The boys were fantastic. They didn't leave me alone for a second. This was a real advantage I had over some of the other runners—they didn't have a crew like I had. For the rest of the way up the pass, the crew took it in 200–300-metre intervals to run with me. They could hardly breathe themselves but they kept right alongside me the whole way.

As the night came in it got really, really cold. It started to snow and it started to blow up a storm. Every 300–400 metres I had to stop and catch my breath. That chair we'd bought all those days ago in Leh was the best thing ever. When I stopped, the lads would put the seat out on the road and I'd sit down. While I was sitting there they'd put clothes on me, take clothes off me, give me my inhaler, get me my nebuliser—you name it, they were there. Each time I'd stop, they'd switch over and one of them walked with me every step of the way. I was so grateful for that moral support—they really weren't doing anything other than being there beside me, and that was all I needed. I can't explain how much their presence helped me.

I was almost hysterical with fear at one point because I couldn't breathe. I'm used to having asthma, but having asthma in a snowstorm, in the dark, at high altitude when you've been out in the elements for 45 hours was something else—it was horrific. And just because it was night-time didn't stop the endless cavalcade of diesel-belching trucks.

As one convoy came through and I felt like I was suffo-
cating, I took a whiff of full-on diesel and just shut down. I
crumpled to the ground and just lay there wondering if I'd
ever get my breath back. The panic made me hyperventilate,
and the hyperventilation made me cry. Chris came over and
patted me on the back and calmed me down. I got to the
point where I could walk again and I picked myself up and
carried on.

On our way up to the top of the pass, we came across a
camp where the road workers obviously lived. In a strange
way it buoyed my spirits, because I thought at least I don't
have to live and work up here. I was doing this because I
chose to—not because I had to.

After six to seven hours of climbing the pass, I thought we
were nearly at the top and I was still stopping every few hundred metres. There was no way I could run so I just shuffled as
quickly as I could. I spent a lot of time trying to calculate how
far I was from the top of the pass. I'd been up there to check out
the lay of the land before the race and I thought I knew the road
pretty well. When I thought I was about 2 kilometres from the
top, Josh took a turn to walk with me. Then he blurted out, 'It's
6 kilometres to the top.' It absolutely killed me. I completely
lost it. Going from thinking I had 2 to go to finding out I had
6 meant two extra hours of climbing in the hideous cold. The
crew were all miserable as hell by that stage, because they'd
been out there for more than 45 hours, too.

The wind had really come up and with the snow as well
conditions were starting to get even more dangerous. It was
at about this time that the race organisers radioed through to
say they were evacuating the pass and that we had to head
back down. Being ordered off the mountain wouldn't mean
the clock would stop though. Whatever time we spent going

down the mountain and coming back up the next day would be included in our race times. I was sitting on my seat in the middle of the storm crying my eyes out. I didn't think I could carry on. I really thought I had nothing left.

The crew were saying to me, 'That's fine, Lisa. You've done everything you can, we've got to get off the mountain. It's too dangerous. Let's go down and come back up tomorrow.' They were wanting to get back down because it was dangerous for them as well.

At this point, Chris came over to me and said, 'No fucking way. You are going to the top. I am not going to let you fail and I am going to stay with you every step of the fucking way. We are not leaving this mountain until you reach the top of that pass. If you leave it now you'll be broken and you won't be able to come back up.'

I looked at him in disbelief. I tried to change his mind. 'I can come back tomorrow and finish it.' But he wasn't having a bar of it.

'You need to reach the top of that pass or you're not going to make it.' He was shaking me and shouting at me, telling me to come back to him. Chris's belief in me and his steadfastness at not letting me fail gave me the motivation to go on. He was saying to me, 'You've been planning this for nine months. You've put everything into this. We've put everything into this. You can't fail now. You've got to get to the top.' So I got up and I took the next step.

I pushed on and the next two hours were hell. But there was no turning back from that point. Chris and Josh never left my side and they got me to the top of the pass. Getting to the top of Tanglang La was pretty much the finish line for me. From the top of the pass there was still 30 kilometres to go, but it was all downhill so I knew that once I got to the top of

Tanglang La I was pretty much finished and nothing would stop me.

At the top of the pass we were all crying with relief that I'd finally made it. I was severely hypothermic by this stage and we had to get off the mountain. There was no way the organisers would let us carry on. They'd been telling us to come down for the past couple of hours and the boys kept telling them we were on our way down, even while we were still heading upwards.

We knew we couldn't stay at the top of the pass so we headed back down to the camp where I'd rested earlier in the day. On the way back down, I was lying in the back seat while the boys tried to keep me warm. They managed to get me in my sleeping bag and keep me awake until we got back to the camp. I was so buzzed out and stoked that I'd made the top of Tanglang La that it was like being on the best drugs ever! I was so happy because I'd given it my all and gone beyond breaking point then carried on some more. It was one of the most special moments of my life.

It took us two hours to drive back down the mountain, then we waited down there for an hour and a a half before spending another two hours driving back up again when the weather cleared. Molly and Sam were behind us and they'd got off the mountain earlier.

Once we got back up to the top of the pass it was still snowing, but by now I didn't really care. We got back up there at about four or five o'clock in the morning and I knocked off the last 30 kilometres. Again, Chris and Josh were with me the whole way. It was still freezing cold and we couldn't breathe properly. I was running down in snow, hail and sleet but I could't have cared less. I didn't care how long it took me to get down there because I knew that I was going to finish. I was so happy.

I knew that Sharon and Ray had both finished but they'd both had huge problems with altitude sickness. They'd both managed to get over the pass before the weather turned bad so they'd done good times. The medical crew had held Ray up at the top of the pass and he was in a bad way. At one point, his crew had gone up ahead and left him and he had ended up running the wrong way. The race organisers were trying to convince him to turn around but he didn't recognise them and he was convinced that they were trying to cut his kidneys out to sell on the black market. While Ray was at the medical checkpoint, Sharon passed him and went on to win the race.

No such problems for me on the downward trail. I finally crossed the finish line with my whole crew. It was an incredibly special moment. Well, for all of us except Luke, the cameraman. He was about to film the most crucial shot of the race, me crossing the line with my crew. About 50 metres from the line, Luke is trying to run alongside us and capture the moment of us running in. Then we hear, 'Aarrrrggghh!' and see Luke sprawling on the ground. In the footage you can see the camera drop and then all you can see is me and the rest of the crew absolutely cracking up laughing. That's how we went across the line— laughing our heads off.

Across the line, there was lots of hugging, kissing and photographs before we all piled back into the car for the six-hour drive back to Leh. Once again, after completing a race I was completely euphoric and absolutely knackered all at the same time. But it's the euphoria I remember. Physically, I was fine. Even with all the highs and the lows, my body wasn't feeling too bad.

The drive back was horrible as we were all crammed into one van. We were all tired and slightly nauseous with the altitude as we climbed back over the pass but nothing could dampen down our excitement at having finished La Ultra and our enthusiasm at the prospect of a cold shower and a bed back at our hotel.

Going back up the pass, Sam and Molly were a few hours behind me. We drove past Sam as she was running down the pass towards the finish line. I got out of the car and gave her a big hug. I assured her she didn't have far to go and that she was going to make it. Just a few hundred metres behind her we stopped again so I could give Molly a hug and reassure her she was close to the finish. All of our crews were yahooing and jumping up and down. The supportive atmosphere was really amazing.

The next day we had the prize-giving and there was one hell of a party. On the very next day was a marathon and a half marathon that had been organised for any local runners or crew members that wanted to run it. Venkat ran the half marathon, which was a bloody good effort given the amount of running he'd done with me and the long hours he'd had to stay awake. But the most surprising contestant in the marathon was none other than Ray Sanchez. I think maybe he wanted to prove himself a little bit, having been beaten by Sharon. The rest of us were looking like death warmed up and there's Ray running a marathon in altitude in under four hours. The man is a machine.

There was no way I would have survived even the first day of La Ultra, let alone 53 hours, 5 minutes and 50 seconds, without my incredible crew. They did everything within their power to make it possible for me to complete this gruelling adventure. Every single step of the way they were there, willing me to the finish. This victory was not mine alone but it belonged to me, my crew and my wonderful sponsors who believed me when I said I could do the highest and toughest ultramarathon in the world.

To Chris, my powerhouse, my motivator, the one who made me pull all the last reserves out of my battered body and my close to broken spirit; to Josh, my passionate fighter, with the determination of steel and the action to back it up; to Venkat, the dad of the crew, the organiser, the smoother of ways; to Luke, the tireless cameraman, the capturer of the drama, and the one who provided the biggest laugh of all at the finish line; to Rana, my smiley, dedicated, tireless crew man and pacer; and to Sunny, who smoothed the way for me from the start, eased my way into India and got me to the start line before having to leave us—I thank you all from the bottom of my heart.

La Ultra The High 2011 results

Sharon Gayter (UK): 37 hours 34 minutes 37 seconds
Ray Sanchez (US): 39 hours 03 minutes 00 seconds
Jason Rita (Australia): 45 hours 55 minutes 05 seconds
Lisa Tamati (New Zealand): 53 hours 05 minutes 50 seconds
Samantha Gash (Australia): 58 hours 15 minutes 20 seconds
Molly Sheridan (US): 58 hours 56 minutes 00 seconds

Kelly's ultra tips

Kelly Sheerin is the manager of the AUT University Running Mechanics Clinic and is an expert in running biomechanics. What follows are some of the key things you need to know to develop a correct running technique. Many of these components are often forgotten in training programs, when the focus is on endurance rather than efficiency.

If you're running a 5-kilometre race you can get away with a lot; because you're longer distance it is essential you have good running technique.

Adopting proper running form and mechanics leads to improved efficiency and economy. You will move forward with greater ease, while burning less energy than you will with poor technique. An efficient, well-balanced running technique also puts less stress on muscles, tendons and bones, which can help you prevent injuries over the many months you will need to train for an ultra.

For more information visit http://running.aut.ac.nz.

Good form starts with maintaining an upright posture. Aim to keep the centre of your head, shoulders, hips, and foot-striking ankle in a vertical line:

Kelly's Ultra Tip 1—avoid leaning forward from the waist,

which often happens when you get fatigued late in long runs. Stand upright as if you're a puppet being controlled by a string.

Kelly's Ultra Tip 2—practise looking down at the road/trail with your eyes, without tilting your head down. When your head tilts forward, the rest of your body will follow.

Your arms should be held at your sides with a loose 90° angle formed at the elbows. Allow your arms to swing in a natural, relaxed pendulum motion from the shoulders, forward and back.

Your arms are the counterbalance to your legs, and just as you should have a balanced stride with your legs, you should also have a balanced arm swing. If your arm swing is different or exaggerated on one side, chances are your lower extremity mechanics are out of kilter, too:

Kelly's Ultra Tip 3—while coming forward your hands should not cross the centre-line of your body, and your shoulders should not rotate from side to side.

Over-striding is a common running fault, caused by stretching out too far in front of your body. This can lead to the promotion of braking forces that will oppose the propulsive forces you are trying to develop with your muscles:

Kelly's Ultra Tip 4—when your foot strikes the ground your knee should be slightly flexed and your foot positioned under, or just in front of, your hips.

The difference between good and poor running mechanics can sometimes be heard. A loud, audible foot strike can be linked to large impact forces, which is usually inefficient and potentially injurious. In contrast, a runner with good form tends to glide along, landing softly on each foot:

Kelly's Ultra Tip 5—listen to your foot strike and try to make it as quiet as possible.

Strength or resistance training is not commonly included

in many endurance-running programs, but it is an essential component to ensure that you can maintain the correct form throughout an ultra-distance run. Running form often degrades rapidly as the stablising muscles of the hips and core become fatigued. Simple, daily functional exercises such as bridges, squats and lunges can help maintain the strength in these key running muscles:

Kelly's Ultra Tip 6—establish a daily routine of simple strengthening exercises that focus on strengthening the hips and core abdominal muscles. Don't cheat on these—always be aware of your posture and form.

The best time to make technique changes is during the off-season, but most runners don't have a true off-season and therefore the best time to make these changes is NOW:

Kelly's Ultra Tip 7—dedicate one run each week to 'technique training' where you focus on correct form.

Lisa's list of ultramarathon events

People quite often ask me which ultra-races are on my bucket list. Here's the list as it stands at the moment. The ones marked with an asterisk are ones that I have competed in.

Australasia
New Zealand
Northburn 100 (http://northburn100.co.nz)
*Around the Mountain (www.mountainrelay.co.nz)
*Te Houtaewa Challenge (www.90milebeachrun.com)

Australia
*The North Face 100 (www2.thenorthface.com.au/100)
The Track Outback Race (www.thetrack-outbackrace.com)

Europe

France/Italy/Switzerland
Ultra-Trail du Mont-Blanc (www.ultratrailmb.com)
La Petite Trotte à Léon (www.ultratrailmb.com)—part of the
    Ultra-Trail du Mont-Blanc that can be raced separately

Greece
Spartathlon (www.spartathlon.gr)

Sweden
The Ice Ultra (www.beyondtheultimate.co)

Africa

Cape Verde
Boavista Ultramarathon (www.boavistaultramarathon.com)

Egypt
*Sahara Race (www.4deserts.com/sahararace)

Kenya
Amazing Maasai Ultra (www.amazingmaasaiultra.org)

Morocco
Marathon des Sables (http://darbaroud.com)

Namibia
The Desert Ultra (www.beyondtheultimate.co)

Niger
*Trans 333 (www.extreme-runner.fr/marathon-desert-gb/333.
php). This race takes place in a different desert every year,
but the year I did it, it was in Niger

South Africa
Comrades Marathon 89 km (www.comrades.com)

Americas
Chile
Atacama Crossing (www.4deserts.com/atacamacrossing)

Peru
The Jungle Ultra (www.beyondtheultimate.co)

United States
Arrowhead 135 (www.arrowheadultra.com)
*Badwater (www.badwater.com)
Hardrock 100 (www.hardrock100.com)
Iditarod Trail Invitational (www.alaskaultrasport.com)
The Mountain Ultra (www.beyondtheultimate.co)
Rio del Lago 100 miler (www.desertskyadventures.com/rdl)
Western States Endurance Run (www.ws100.com)

Antarctica
The Last Desert (www.4deserts.com/thelastdesert)

Asia
China
*Gobi March (www.4deserts.com/gobimarch)

India
*La Ultra The High (www.thehigh.in)

Acknowledgements

Lisa Tamati

A huge thankyou to everyone who has supported me over the past few years.

The Himalaya support crew for getting me through the tough times: Chris Ord, Josh Paurini, Venkat Krishnan, Luke McNee, Ranjit Singh Phagura and Sunny Grewal.

My best mates and crews from the NZ Run and Death Valley: Megan Stewart, Nadene George, Jason Obirek, Mitchell Tamati, Howard Dell, Chris Cruikshank, Gerhard Lusskandl, Jill Danoon, and my parents, Cyril and Isobel Tamati.

My amazing sponsors and supporters:

Stephen Winnacott—The North Face

Mike and Rachel Perrett—Chillaxing

Jeff and Angely Roby—Butch Pet Foods

Murray Dick—Taranaki Engineering

The team at City Fitness

The team at Bartercard

Deepak Ahluwahlia—ETL Group Ltd

Jim Bedwell—Red 8

The team at Thompson's Nutrition

Ross Fanthorpe—Govett Quillam Lawyers

Sonny Fernando—Efinity

Max Bound—Accounting 2001

Hayden Pohio—Manuka Boosta

Mike Brewer—Taranaki Newspapers

Jaron Mumby—Fire Design

Phil Kingsley Jones

The team at Juice Plus

The team at Nalu Productions

Kylie Sousa

Sheryl Hewlett

Terry David

Tom Pinckney—Northburn Station

Glen Christiansen—Golden Gate Lodge

Will Hinchcliff—EECP

Harry Duynhoven—New Plymouth Mayor

Ian Mckellar

Peggy Schwieters

Kim Bachelor

Victoria Bachelor

Dean Karnazes

Jennifer Steinman

Nicola McCloy

I would like to give my warmest thanks to:

Cyril and Isobel Tamati, for always making me feel right at home in New Plymouth.

Nadene George, Megan Stewart, Rajat Chauhan, Virginia Winstone, Tracey Woodford, Ben Winrow and Kelly Sheerin for sharing their experiences and expertise.

Michael Dall-Hjorring, Valerie Henderson and Rick Laird for their invaluable advice on what runners want to read.

My most excellent colleagues at Allen & Unwin, especially Kathryn Knight in Sydney and the team in Auckland.

Fiona McRae for her consummate editing skill.

Angela Dall-Hjorring, Beris Forde, Katy Yiakmis, Tree La

Rooy, Kim Buchanan, Michelle Hayward, Sue Lewis and Team Invy for their ongoing support.

And, of course, Lisa, without whom I wouldn't own a pair of running shoes, much less actually use them!